GOVERNANCE
BUHARI'S
WAY

MISAPPLICATION *of the* LEADERSHIP PRAXIS

DR. ANTHONY OBI OGBO

AMERICAN
JOURNAL *of*
TRANSFORMATIONAL
LEADERSHIP

In a complex economy, installing a leader without relevant skills is like hiring a tailor to an Intensive Care Unit to perform surgery, just because he can handle needle and thread.

Dr. Anthony Obi Ogbo

 American Journal *of* Transformational Leadership

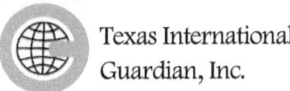 Texas International Guardian, Inc.

AMERICAN JOURNAL *of*
TRANSFORMATIONAL LEADERSHIP

Texas International Guardian Newspapers Inc.
© 2016 All rights reserved.
CreateSpace Independent Publishing Platform.
ISBN-13: 978-1532865350
ISBN-10: 153286535X
Printed in the United States of America (USA).

Cover design, book design, and production *by*
Anthony Obi Ogbo, *International Guardian*

*Bequeathed to Nigerian leaders,
now, and in generations to come.*

Appreciation

I am a strong believer in the adage, 'It takes a village,' therefore
special thanks must go to all those who have contributed
physically and emotionally to the success of this publication;
Dr. Chris Ulasi, Dr. Rita Ogbo-Kingsley,
Dr. Anthony Kingsley, Chief Chris Ogbo, Paul Nwokedi,
Joe Nwokedi, Stephanie Adaeze Ogbo,
Anthony Obieze Ogbo, and Isaac Chibueze Ogbo;
Lady Laura Ekume, and Dr. Emeaba Emeaba.
Also thanks to Dr. Olayinka Dixon-Oludaiye, and
the editorial staff of *Texas International Guardian Newspapers* for
exceptional editorial assistance.

Regards,
Anthony Obi Ogbo

Foreword

BY DR OLAYINKA DIXON-OLUDAIYE,
PHD, CIPM, MPM

In his last book, *The Influence of Leadership*, a research study, Dr. Anthony Obi Ogbo, leadership and
management scholar explored how the political, cultural,
social, and economic conditions in Nigeria influence the
lives of Nigerian citizens through lived experiences of
two citizens from each of the six geopolitical regions of
the country. The research centered on people (Nigerian
citizens), through the subjects of management and leadership, and through the processes of managing and leading.

Dr. Ogbo made substantial recommendations for
leaders, which focused primarily on the themes
categorized as moral philosophy, organizational change,

transformation, and diversity management. These remedies, Dr. Ogbo contended, could help the present and aspiring leaders to develop effective leadership strategies to manage their citizens, public service system, and resources.

Governance Buhari's Way is consistent with Dr. Ogbo's exploration of solutions to the dysfunctional system presently operating in Nigeria. While the content critiques the styles and philosophy of the Nigerian President, Muhammadu Buhari, Dr. Ogbo researched and discussed some applicable models relevant to leadership behavior and practice, to deliver a structure for effective management of Nigeria, its people, and its abundant resources.

As Dr. Ogbo noted, this book is not a condemnation of Nigeria's struggle for survival, but an academic work about the misuse of leadership in a democratic setting, and a foundationally intrinsic misunderstanding of leadership as against management structures. Using relevant concepts, the book appraised President Buhari's apparent and reactionary temperament in handling the affairs of government, and considers how ill-informed choices or errors in judgement might derail Nigeria's quest for unity.

The book, *Governance Buhari's Way*, cited incompati-

bility in President Buhari's executive structure, catego-
rizing them into three groups, "fanatics who worship
him; cohorts who think they understand him; and underhanded politicians who have lied that they know him."
On how an alliance between President Buhari and his incompatible cohorts would inspire a progressive change,
the book invoked the interchangeable roles of the managing, and the leading, in the public service system - setting the records straight on the use of, so called,
technocrats in running the public system.

The organization of this book centers on a literature
review of significant concepts of transformation management. Besides a discussion on the language of leadership, the book reviewed the application of moral
philosophy in the governance system; the process of organizational transformation, and the philosophy of the
change process. These concepts were adequately applied
in appraising President Buhari's unconventional style of
leadership within a democratic system of government.
They also underscore major reasons why his regime appears currently shaky, and might be headed for the
worst, without an immediate structured intervention.

The Author's writing approach in this book is unique -
a mixture of academic language and conventional con-
versational humor. However, the facts, suppositions, and

recommendations remain a scholarly composition of the science of "how not to manage people and resources". As Dr. Ogbo put it, "In a complex economy, installing a leader without relevant skills is like hiring a tailor to an Intensive Care Unit (ICU) to perform surgery, just because they can handle needle and thread." In all, this book is an absolutely illuminating and interesting piece of work.

TABLE *of*
Contents

III

THE HOMECOMING ■ Page 45

IV

FINAL THOUGHTS ■ Page 97

CONCEPTS AND THEORIES

■ There has to be a reason why, with all the attention accorded to the study of leadership and management, organizational challenges still overwhelm accomplishments. As key objectives in this book, communication of theories would be clear in addressing the comprehension of tough challenges which leaders must address in the 21st century.

ONE

Composition of this Book

■ This is basically a book on leadership, and relevant tools to appropriately lead people, resources, and the connecting elements. Using issues in Nigeria as yardsticks, the chapters invoke fundamental concepts in effective leadership, and explain the intellectual and physical competence of the leader.

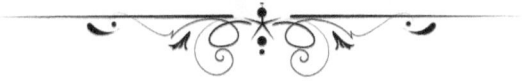

The Book

The problem used to be just the dictators – some inglorious army dissidents unable to differentiate between the constitution and a loaded gun; their intemperance for power, and of course their inability to live up to the core

Buhari - 1985 and now. **There is a wide demarcation between human ideology and personal outfit - for a change in attire has no connection, whatsoever, with individual traits or demeanor.**
Photo: International Guardian/Archives.

tests of leadership. Today the problem has shifted to a confused populace with short memories, who are unable to identify their predators and permanently keep them away from coming back to rule their ruins. Based on relevant concepts of leadership and art of leading, this book renders a paradigmatic appraisal of President Buhari; his personality, temperament and leadership philosophies; related rudiments of his past tyrannical stewardship; and how deceptively, he might thoughtlessly punctuate a hard-fought progress Nigeria has made in attaining a united nation.

This book is not a reading novel; it is neither a rhythmical composition of talking-points for inspirational speakers, nor a campaign manual for either the political aspirants or consultants. Whereas all of the above entities may find the content useful at specific capacities, it is basically a book on leadership, and relevant tools to appropriately lead people, resources, and the connecting elements. Using issues in Nigeria as yardsticks, the chapters invoke fundamental concepts in effective leadership, and explain the intellectual and physical competence of the leader.

The Leader

The content of this book focuses on Muhammadu Buhari, the President of Nigeria who took office on May 29, 2015. It is a scholarly exploration of the misapplica-

tion of the concepts of leadership in the executive structure: a practice that has largely grounded Nigeria's attainment of socio-political and economic resurgence.
Based on relevant concepts of leadership and art of leading, this book renders a paradigmatic appraisal of President Buhari; his personality, temperament and leadership
philosophies; related rudiments of his past tyrannical
stewardship; and how currently he is handling matters of
governance in a democratic system – a setting that might
be strange to his ideology. Some passages in this book
would decode President Buhari's applied and intellectual
competence through knowledge and leadership assessment of his personality traits, his governance approach,
and recent political engagements.

Traumatized by the intricacies of an unfulfilled dream
of Islamic statehood, Muhammadu Buhari, for a second
time, has swaggered into the leadership suite of Africa's
most populous country with three categories of followers: fanatics who worship him; cohorts who think they
understand him; and underhanded politicians who have
lied that they know him. Could an alliance between this
autocrat and a team of incompatible cohorts inspire progressive change?

There is a wide demarcation between human ideology
and personal outfit - for a change in attire has no connection, whatsoever, with individual traits or demeanor.
Buhari was a soldier to the core, and had spent his entire

career in the military, facilitating wars and instigating coups. In his career as a soldier, he was no *Colin Powell**, by any means. He was one of those Nigerians whose tribal and zonal connections favorably took him to the top, with little or no prerequisite for educational achievement or excellence of mental attitude. He remained in the Army, received substantial training enough to load a riffle and aim at a basic target.

Now a civilian, most electorates saw him differently. His presidential campaign handlers portrayed him as a refurbished dictator who gradually (or, even, dramatically) metamorphosed to a transformational leader. But leadership traits are engrained in ideology - definitely not through a change in attire from combat gears to traditional robes and designer suits. Thus, this book focuses more on President Muhammadu Buhari's first brush with democratic governance; his application of leadership in the executive structure: a systematic appraisal of his philosophies, and how his approach so far may not bring forth an anticipated change.

Cheering this President into power may also reveal the devastations of a confused populace; their reluctance

---

Colin Luther Powell, a Commander of the U.S. Army Forces Command (1989) and a Chairman of the Joint Chiefs of Staff (1989–1993) retired as a four-star general in the United States Army. He later became the first African American to serve as the United States Secretary of State, serving under U.S. President George W. Bush from 2001 to 2005.

to learn from the past, and their unwillingness to separate emotions and political interests from the realities of
a long-term pursuit for a united nation. Thoughts expressed in this book may serve as a true revelation that
political interests and "national cakes" are perishable,
whereas a good governance structure goes a long way.

Concepts

Contemporary leaders are equipped with transformational competencies, including knowledge and skills,
personality values, confidence, expertise, influence
strategies, and essential behaviors to accomplish tasks
and overcome fundamental challenges in modern leadership. How does President Buhari's ideology harmonize
the relevant concepts and theories about change management? This book explains Nigeria's dysfunctional system, while it also explores some applicable concepts to
deliver a framework for effective management of the nation, its people, and its resources.

President Buhari had run a campaign based on the
'change' mantra. Whereas the core content of the book
focuses on practical and intellectual valuation of his
stewardship, the chapters unleash the language of effective governance through conceptual frameworks con-
comitant with constructive theories of leadership. This
book explains the mechanics of managing change in a
complex economy. It invokes the dialect of transforma-

tion management to communicate the demands of moral philosophy, technology innovation, demographics, and the team process in effective governance.

Core theoretical concepts* that would guide matters and solutions discussed in this book are;

- ***Knowledge, dialect, and praxis of leadership:*** Just like a tribal leader and his knowledge of his disciples, territory, and language; a good organizational leader must understand the vernaculars of leadership, and speak them without a foreign accent.

- ***Demands of moral philosophy:*** The application of this concept in strong issues of governance requires relevant competence and approach. As a branch of philosophy, ethics explores the scope of moral values. Moral philosophy therefore addresses specific standards, rules, and values that regulate the practice of right or wrong.

- ***The transformation mantra:*** The most fundamental stage of any governance initiative is to strategically determine its existing state, and to evaluate progress which enables it build a solid foundation for future developments.

---

*A concept marker must be clarified by theoretical meaning. Concepts are basic building blocks of scientific theory. Discussions in this book are corroborated by a review of literature of relevant concepts. The goal is to communicate unambiguousness, and present concrete results that may be tested and evaluated by others.

- *The philosophy of change:* Organizational change is a transformation process from the present to projected future state in order to galvanize relevant growth. This process could only be effective when leaders understand the technicalities that imbue the process.

TWO

Concepts and theories

The study composition of this book was guided by a theoretical framework that included Moral Philosophy, Organizational Transformation and the Change Philosophy.

The Leadership Praxis:
Knowledge and Dialect

Thomas Wren, in his work, *Insights on Leadership through the Ages*, identified leadership from an approach that harmonizes the context of this book. According to *Wren*, the sensation of leadership is complex, and often involves the persistent collaboration of the leader, the followers, and the surrounding circum-stances. A leader must therefore, understand the charac-teristics and interaction of these three indispensable elements in order to function effectively. Similar to *Wren, Afsaneh Nahavandi* acknowledged the differences and complexities in the meaning of leadership, but of-fered three common elements in communicating a defi-nition;

- *Group phenomenon*, reflecting the interactions of the leader and followers.
- *Goal directed and action oriented phenomenon*, reflecting role play and influence.
- *The practice of leading,* involving hierarchical structure within a group.

Gary Yukl also provided a clear analysis about the ambiguities in the definition of leadership, and offered a framework that combines traits, behaviors, influence, in-teraction patterns, role relationships, and occupation of a managerial position.

Whereas the art of managing and leading were some-times used interchangeably to explain specific matters in this book, *John Kotter*, cautioned that leadership must at all times be separated from management because the two are radically different. *Kotter's* explanation made sense. Whereas Management helps individuals to pro-duce projected products and services of dependable quality, at a specific budget, leadership aims at taking the organization into the future, creating and exploiting opportunities. Leadership according to *Kotter*, deals with creating vision, producing useful change, and managing people and their behaviors.

With hundreds of other definitions however, and with more being created progressively, most leadership gurus would attest that "leadership" is the most studied but least understood discipline in our learning core curriculum. Therefore, there has to be a reason why, with all the attention accorded to the study of leadership and management, organizational challenges still overwhelm accomplishments. As key objectives in this book, communication of theories would be clear in addressing the comprehension of tough challenges which leaders must address in the 21st century.

Using issues of Nigeria's governance impairment as a measure, discussions in this book reflect the thorough knowledge, dialect, and the praxis of leadership according to President Buhari. Misapplication and laxity in operational standards would be unveiled, whereas recommendations would be adequately offered for performance effectiveness.

The dialect of modern governance in a democratic setting symbolizes an innovative attitude to organizational transformation. It might reflect the leadership trends in the present-day society. In Nigeria, a region where the practice of democracy is still a luxury, the dialect and practice of modern-day effective leadership could be based on hope, aspiration, and performance standards. To meet these challenges, present and aspiring Nigerian leaders must be equipped with transformational individualities, including personality standards, self-assurance, expertise, influence tactic, and the proper behaviors to inspire change.

The language of modern leadership must reflect and address imminent challenges facing the people, especially in Nigeria where multiplicity of tribes intensify the burden of national unity. This book adequately subjects President Buhari's leadership style into a systematic watch, identifying significant lapses, dissecting their impacts in attaining progress, and recommending different approaches for performance success.

While President Buhari fiddles with hard-hitting matters of his executive practice – holding his nation to economic hostage with claims of organizational transformation, the phenomenological reality projects him more as an unapproachable ruler. In the current era of diversity in tribes and tongues, the Chief Executive must communicate, without faltering, the core values of transformational leadership. He must be an innovative trailblazer, passionate about the plight of the people, and serious about his missions and aspirations of a united nation. As *Kotter* noted, such a leader must inspire change, motivate subordinates and carry them along toward the finishing line of immeasurable possibilities and success.

It must be noted that Nigeria's success as a nation hangs on the potentials of the three arms of the governance system - the executive, legislature, and judiciary - to rise up to their constitutional responsibilities. However, leadership demands more than constitutional obligations, and could encompass developing a strong vision; motivating an organizational structure of innovation and transformation; and committing to a strategic plan for performance accomplishment. Could President Buhari wisely engage subordinates who understand this dialect, or will he continue to parade submissive cohorts who could only carry his briefcases and lick his boots?

The study composition of this book was guided by a theoretical framework that included Moral Philosophy, Organizational Transformation, and the Change Philosophy:

Demands of Moral Philosophy

One major trait with President Buhari in his rule as a dictator, is his advocacy for a clean society; his push to cleanse Nigeria from a malodorous corrupt culture. His approach may have been either unscholarly or tainted with retributive tendencies, but the truth is that Nigeria's governance structure has been troubled with a high level of corruption, especially in the public service system. Since its independence in 1960 till date, Nigeria has

been cursed with dishonest leaders unable to differentiate between their tribes and their constituencies; unable
to separate their wallets from the national treasury; and
worse, incompetent to face the challenges of the tide.
Therefore, Buhari's push for an immaculate ethical system must be applauded as a good try.

However, the application of this concept in strong issues of governance requires relevant competence and
approach. As a branch of philosophy, ethics explores the
scope of moral values. Moral philosophy therefore addresses specific standards, rules, and values which regulate the practice of right or wrong. This would entail the
regulation of individual conduct to avoid doing harm to
others. This is why a good knowledge of the foundation
of ethical decision-making reasoning can positively af-
fect the political process. Thus, the advocacy for a thorough application of moral philosophy in the Nigeria's
system must not be seen as disdain of the regime, but as
an inevitable task to properly infuse trust and transparency into the population.

The Transformation Mantra

The most fundamental stage of any governance initiative is to strategically determine its existing state and
evaluate progress that enables it build a solid foundation
for future developments. President Buhari, his campaign
team, and indeed his party, the All Progressive Congress

(APC) were right in their adoption of the "Change" paradigm as a campaign theme. From all ramifications, Nigeria needed a paradigm shift as an antidote to its governance catastrophe. Paradigm shift should not be seen as a reshuffle of the cabinet. *Thomas Kuhn*, an American physicist, historian, and philosopher, in his historic book, **The Structure of Scientific Revolutions* defined 'Paradigm Shift' as a change from one way of thinking to another; a transformation revolution driven by the agents of change to appropriately position an organization for a better future.

Is Buhari a transformational leader? Does he possess the demeanor of a leader? A leader serious about any transformation agenda must generate the necessary excitement to revitalize his constituency. He must develop a strategic communication of clear vision - a goal, an agenda, and set up a powerful apparatus for performance appraisal. So how had these values harmonize Buhari's individuality?

The Philosophy of Change

R. G. Coawin in a research study about strategies for

---

*Thomas S. Kuhn's work, *The Structure of Scientific Revolutions* (1962; second edition 1970) was a landmark publication that inspires a successful dialogue in the scholarly communities about the realities of history, philosophy, and sociology of scientific knowledge. Kuhn's signature term for transformation revolution, "paradigm shift", has since become an English-language idiom.

innovation made a great case for developing a change philosophy toward an organizational growth. To inspire relevant sociological strategies for organizational reform and effectiveness, *Coawin* postulated that an organization could be more easily changed if it is invaded by liberal, creative, and unconventional outsiders with fresh perspectives. How do Buhari and his cabinet fit into this category? How does a recycling of untrusted public officers with records of embezzlement of public funds harmonize the tenets of paradigmatic revolution?

Amidst multifaceted global economic challenges, managing the demands of organizational change could be dependent on the leaders and their zeal to properly facilitate the process. As noted earlier, "Change" must not be seen as a cabinet reshuffle, or a mass retrenchment of employees; neither does it necessitate a mass arrest of individuals suspected of bribery and corruption.

Organizational change is a transformation process from the present to the projected future state, to galvanize relevant growth. This approach could only be effective when leaders understand the technicalities that imbue the process. Leaders therefore must be armed with strategies to confront significant complications and create adequate machineries to mitigate change-related hindrances.

THE UNHEEDED WARNING SIGNS

■ For an ex-soldier who once overthrew with a loaded riffle, the very constitution he now pretends to be defending, the ideals of representative governance might be in jeopardy.

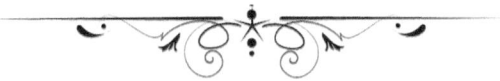

THREE

Between democracy and antiquated cruelty

■ The presidential race, at some point, transcended beyond a push to shove the incumbent, but rather, a contention between the survival of Nigeria's democracy and Buhari's antiquated cruelty.

October 15, 2014, Nigeria's former military ruler, Muhammadu Buhari declared he would contest for office of the Nigerian President. In his declaration, he criticized the incumbent President Goodluck Jonathan and his administration for leading a corrupt legacy and failing to tackle the Boko Haram Islamist insurgency.

Buhari ran as presidential candidate for All Progressives Congress (APC) - the major opposition contender while President Jonathan remained the flag bearer for the People's Democratic Party (PDP) in a race that set the print, electronic, and social media agog with commentaries regarding electioneering promises, political prospects, and executive competence.

Buhari, who at some point battled with issues relating to age and health, had been involved (one way or the other), in every Nigerian military rule since the civil war. He had participated in coups; and as a retired junta member, he had run three presidential races without a scrap of success. His thread of losses posed a major concern for most undecided voters. For instance, in 2003 he lost the presidential election to incumbent Olusegun Obasanjo and refused to concede. Again, in 2007 he failed woefully in the presidential polls against the late president Yar'Adua and took his protest to court. Thereafter, in 2011, he again, lost the presidential election to President Jonathan and headed to the court houses for another failed miracle.

Jonathan, on the other hand, was being accused of associating with a political party that had ruled the country for about 16 years with little or nothing to show as groundbreaking accomplishments. He was dubbed "clueless" by his opposition, who claimed that this incumbent sightlessly surrounded himself with dishonest and selfish allies while he hopelessly and haplessly grappled with matters of governance. Buhari's handlers campaigned under the "Change" mantra, calling for a total overhaul of the status quo.

The opposition's arguments were substantial. However the thing that kept brothering Nigerians and perhaps the international community was that anytime Buhari lost a race, thousands of lives perished through uncontrolled violence, lynching of humans, and burning of churches. Nigerians were worried that Buhari, since his removal as a dictator, had not given up on his quest for this topmost position. His regime as a dictator, December 1983 through August 1985, was very short and did not give the dictator any chance to transform Nigeria's governmental system the way he wanted, into a Taliban-modeled structure where the Islamic Sharia laws would suppress the judicial process.

To ease voters' fears, Buhari, in campaign trips to most Christian states denied allegations of repression. Simultaneously, in a series of interviews with the *BBC Hausa*, Buhari vehemently stood his grounds on his jihadist values. He, in fact, shocked the nation when he advocated total and unflinching support, including an amnesty for the terrorism group, Boko Haram. His suspected advocacy for Boko Haram was reignited when the group named him, at the time, as the envoy in their proposed dialogue with the government. These were all factual information that the voters apparently scorned during the heated electioneering era.

The presidential race, at some point, transcended beyond a push to shove the incumbent, but rather, a contention between the survival of Nigeria's democracy and Buhari's antiquated cruelty. For instance, in his retributive rule as dictator, he projected himself as a Roman god, and ruled like the Taliban. Yet many Nigerian voters claimed they knew this ex-dictator and argued his incorruptibility, basing their beliefs from doctored information retrieved from *Google** and *Wikipedia***.

It would be worth knowing that Nigerians who were 52 years in 2014 were barley one year old when Muhammadu Buhari joined the army in 1962. Yet he had remained one of the few officers without basic education, but who wrangled their way to the barracks as commissioned officers. Many of such officers used their military training to wrestle legitimate power out of the system, rather than defend the country's security needs.

---

*_Google,_ well-known Internet-search domain is an American global technology firm specializing in Internet-related services and products such as online advertising technologies, computing, and software.

** _Wikipedia_ is a content Internet encyclopedia, available to the public who can access the site, and can edit most of its articles. Wikipedia is one of the most popular websites with an extensive wide-ranging reference work.

Buhari's jihadist Islamic ideologies had signaled a dangerous warning to the populace. In my published documentary of Buhari's adventures into the Nigeria's leadership suite, I expressed the disparaging nature of his religious views as a threat to a united nation. I indicated that Buhari was one of those conservative Muslim fanatics with the heart of *Hamas*, a propensity equaling those of **Al Qaeda*, and the vision of the ***Taliban*. He represented those who would question God for creating any being other than a Muslim; or even challenge Him for creating women. To Buhari, gender consideration is a western movie, and women should be perpetually confined to purdah.

Yet Buhari's supporters stood solidly behind him, and would argue on a failed Jonathan's regime as a justification for a Buhari comeback. They had a point too. The security situation in the country had deteriorated, leaving most parts of the North vulnerable to the exploits of

---

Hamas (Ḥarakat al-Muqāwamah al-'Islāmiyyah Islamic Resistance Movement) is a Palestinian Sunni-Islamic fundamentalist organization opposed to Israel's existence in any form. Hamas stresses jihad as the sole and immediate means to solve the problem of Palestine. Hamas aims to create an Islamic state in all of Palestine.

**Al Qaeda* is a rebellious Sunni Islamist global organization founded in 1988 with a network made up of Islamic extremist, Salafist jihadists; designated as a terrorist group by the United Nations Security Council, the North Atlantic Treaty Organization (NATO), the European Union, the United States, Russia, India, and various other countries.

***Taliban* is an Islamic fundamentalist political movement that held power in Afghanistan from 1996 to 2001 and enforced a strict but torturing Islamic law opposed by the international community and leading Muslims countries.

the Boko Haram terror group. Jonathan's campaign, on the other, accused the opposition of instigating violence in the North and using statistics of casualties for political campaigns. But the truth remained, that the race went beyond "competency trial" of the incumbent.

While Nigerians prepared for the presidential polls, voters were advised in another discourse, to articulate a validation that the war to secure Nigeria was not against Islam, but a decisive advocacy where decent culture would override antiquated cruelty; a mission engrained in commonsense to secure a united nation where superiority of tribe, religion, or geographical location would be subdued under one law and common identity.

To succeed as a nation, Nigerians were consistently warned to focus on encouraging the incumbent to fix the structures, instead of supporting the same uniformed mobsters who once prolonged their attainment of economic and socio-political resurgence with authoritative decrees and loaded rifles. Was this warning heeded?

FOUR
The unheeded warning signs

■ An editorial warned that Nigeria could not afford the same dictator twice; that Nigeria could not sanely embrace the same brainless despots that wrecked its national prospects with outmoded military tanks and grenades.

There were three categories of people who sang and danced behind Muhammadu Buhari as he swaggered for a second time, into the leadership suite of Africa's most populous country. The fanatics who worshiped him were too sightless to study his ideology. The cohorts

who thought they understood him were rather suscepti-
ble to electioneering campaign deceit. The desperate but
underhanded politicians who lied that they knew him
just did so, to pave way for their own selfish interests.
Today, one terrible thing that is haunting the current
Nigeria's governance system is an alliance between
Buhari's eccentricity and these incompatible groups of
obsequious cohorts. For an ex-soldier who once overthrew with a loaded riffle, the very constitution he now
pretends to be defending, the ideals of representative
governance might be in jeopardy.

Nigerians were warned by those who understood the
country's system, about Buhari's leadership style; his
personality, and administrative demeanor. It may be recalled that so many stories and commentaries were writ-
ten, analyzing appropriate chances for both candidates,
the incumbent, President Jonathan and General Buhari.

President Jonathan had been President of Nigeria
since 2010. Before then, he served as the Governor of
Bayelsa State from 2005 to 2007, and as the Vice-Presi-
dent of Nigeria from 2007 to 2010. He was a liberal
who launched numerous programs, including that which
transformed the structure of Nigeria's governance. President Jonathan inspired a collective involvement of all
Nigerian zones at all demographic standards to facilitate
unity and faster growth. General Buhari, on the contrary, was a dictator who led a military coup that over-

threw the democratically elected government of President Shehu Shagari in December 31, 1983. The coup terminated Nigeria's short-lived Second Republic which started in 1979.

Less than two weeks to this election, both parties had intensified their campaign with so much information - both related and unrelated to major issues at stake - leaving most voters confused about their interests with both candidates. This author, in an editorial in the *International Guardian,* simplified basic facts related to crucial socio-political issues at stake. In the most comprehensive language, Nigerians were informed on why a continuance of the incumbent for a second and final four-year term would draw them closer to their socio-political freedom and economic prosperity as compared to the APC's opposition squad.

To proceed with this composition, Nigerians were reminded that the damage done by a long thread of military dictatorships that pervaded the country's political history was enormous, and could not have been entirely revamped in just a few democratic tenures. Therefore, going back to those who led those carnages as desirable remedies would be a senseless option.

While both campaigns of President Jonathan and General Buhari were busy swarming the media networks with promotional materials of achievements and manifestos, voters were again reminded that this election was no longer about parties, tribes, or zones of origin, but about two candidates running on contrasting ideologies namely: An antiquated ideology of the ex-dictators and the contemporary ideology a new democratic Nigeria.

The message sounded biased, but emitted the reality that Buhari represented Nigeria's past misery - a dark moment of its history which had officially been confined to the museums. In a sharp contrast, the message alluded to President Jonathan as a valuable incumbent with a mission consistent with long-term transformation possibilities.

Whichever way this editorial might have sounded, it warned that Nigeria could not afford the same dictator twice; that Nigeria could not sanely embrace the same brainless despots that wrecked its national prospects with outmoded military tanks and grenades. To make it crystal clear - the editorial advised that an uninterrupted continuation of the present regime of President Jonathan would not just be a civic duty, but an ancestral call to embrace a new Nigeria, in order to create an environment in which the political godfathers, ex-dictators, and political oppressors would be rendered redundant. A process that could have created the needed opportunities for more qualified Nigerians to totally wrestle their country back from the vandals that once abused it.

FIVE

Playing poker with voter ID

■ From all valuations, the take away of the past presidential race was Professor Jega; his poor supervision, process unpreparedness, suspicious partisan engagements, a lack of transparency, and his courage to lie to his country.

February 14, 2015 - also the Valentine's day - was the initial designated date for the Nigeria's general election. Ordinarily, the atmosphere would have been grounded by activities of the ballot over a traditional Valentine's jolliness, and also, the streets would have been locked down by the engagements of the presidential poll. However, a fluctuating thread of situations changed all that, giving the Valentine its rightful space, and moving the election weeks further. The Independent National Electoral Commission (INEC), had no choice when it decided to move the national elections (Presidential and National Assembly) to March 28th, and the state (Governorship and State Assembly) to April 11th.

When these changes were announced by the INEC's Chairman, Professor Attahiru M. Jega, at a press conference, February 7, media outlets bombarded their readers, listeners, and viewers with countless analysis. The blogs, especially the self-authenticated "i-report" loudhailers blew the issue out of the ordinary, alluding process improprieties on the part of the government. The condemnation of INEC's action got worse – to the extent that John Kerry, the United States Secretary of State issued a release expressing deep disappointment, urging that the Nigerian government not use security concerns as a "pretext" for impeding the democratic process.

Another spectacular thing about this election was that the facts about the controversial postponement were immediately vindicated. There was no way the election could have been held on this day. Besides revelations that the security preparation were insufficient, the major problem was the election process readiness.

Professor Jega may have mislead his country when he

claimed that he was prepared for the polls. Here was Jega (publicly) advocating for a February 14 election date prior to the postponement;

> *"For the things under the commission's control, our accomplishments are to such a degree that we can conduct the election, in spite of the identifiable challenges."*

Now here was the same Jega (again, later) reporting on the commission's distribution of the most important instrument of the process, the Voter ID;

> *"As at 5th February 2015, the total number of Permanent Voter Cards (PVC) collected was 45, 829, 808, representing 66.58% of the total number of registered voters."*

Also alarming was the contrasting figures of the Voter ID distribution among regions at the time of the postponement. Figures released by INEC indicated over-whelmingly, a greater success in the northern region as compared to the south. The breakdown (of distribution), were as follows:

North-West: 80.18%,
North-East: 81.09%,
North-Central 69.89%,
South-East 59.22%,
South-South: 66.66%,
South-West 43.15%.

The critical question, therefore was: If it took Jega

and INEC almost four years to provide voter IDs to only 66.58% of eligible voters, how could the remaining 33.42% eligible voters be assured of IDs in less than 8 days before the Election Day? Even with these despicable figures, Jega continued his acclamation of an impeccable readiness, and bragged about system effectiveness. In his own words, here was Jega;

> "Compared with the 2011 general elections, for instance, our systems are definitely more robust now. Among others, we have gently improved registered voters, having removed over four million multiple registrants; voters will use Permanent Voter Cards (PVCs); and accreditation using card readers will reduce the likelihood of fraud."

This twisting of facts thus raised other issues related to INEC's leadership and trustworthiness; and incited strong disapproval from various groups. For instance, the Southern Nigerian Peoples Assembly (SNPA), an organization of some Southern Nigerian elders, called for Jega's expulsion, accusing the INEC boss of reportedly directing the release of Voter IDs to Emirs, District Heads, and top politicians but not to the voters. This was to allow individual voters multiple IDs and give them rigging opportunities for the opposition candidate, Muhammadu Buhari.

Additionally, SNPA claimed in a press conference,

that Jega met with select leaders of the Northern Elders Forum, led by Prof. Ango Abdullahi, on the 20th August 2014, where strategies for instating a President from the North by all means necessary were discussed and finalized.

States Secretary, Kerry may have also reacted too soon - acting without adequate information from reliable agencies from the United States monitoring the developments. For example, shortly after Kerry's press release, the National Democratic Institute (NDI), a United States nonpartisan organization working to support and strengthen democratic institutions worldwide, in collaboration with International Republican Institute (IRI), issued their report contradicting the secretary's position on the issue.

The NDI/IRI* report expressed concerns that millions of PVCs were not distributed by INEC. Even as INEC indicated plans to move the PVC distribution from Local Government Areas (LGA) down to towns and villages,

---

* *Both the NDI and IRI are based in the United States.*

NDI - *National Democratic Institute* is a nonprofit, nonpartisan organization working to support and strengthen democratic institutions worldwide through citizen participation, openness and accountability in government. The group promote openness and accountability in government by building political and civic organizations, safeguarding elections, and promoting citizen participation. (www.ndi.org).

IRI - *International Republican Institute*, encourages democracy in places where it is absent, and helps democracy become more effective where it is in danger, by bringing government closer to citizens, making it a responsive, transparent, effective institution. (www.iri.org).

the report indicated that the exercise did not commence. To further corroborate allegations of Jega's imprecise motive, the report stated that in some states, the distribution exercise was repeatedly postponed at some locations, leading to further erosion of trust in the INEC.

Jega's preparations were so messy that at the time of the new election dates, some Nigerians were still unsure whether a voter without a PVC, but whose name was on the register, would be allowed to vote on election day, and what arrangements were being put in place to adjudge such matters.

With all these developments, it became clear that the major issue about the entire election was Jega; his doubtful motives, and his level of readiness. Thousands of eligible voters took to the streets of various towns in the south where President Jonathan had a greater edge over his contender to protest non availability of Voter ID cards. The major implication remained unquestionable: that voters from the south were collectively marginalized.

SIX

Jonathan's self-inflicted wounds and supervisory blindness

■ In the very conservative Nigeria's learning community, celebrating a self-inflicted failure is inconceivable. Why would anybody idolize a loser for doing just about what any loser would do – admit and accept his loss? For goodness sake, why would anyone glorify a leader who erred, lost, gave up, and ran off?

The mere fact that a sitting President and his first lady could not pass the card-accreditation process they initiated, should indicate that the election was destined for disaster. The incumbent President and presidential can-

didate of the People's Democratic Party, Goodluck
Ebele Jonathan, and his First Lady, Patience, were declined by the card reader at his home town, Otuoke in
Bayelsa State. This caused the whole accreditation
process that preceded Nigeria's 2015 general election to
draw mixed reactions.

The crux of the matter was that, Professor Attahiru
Jega, to whom President Jonathan entrusted the electoral
sector, the Independent National Electoral Commission
(INEC), could no longer be trusted with supervision. A
thread of events that occurred before a postponement of
the initial ballot date clearly revealed that the INEC boss
might have been compromised to rig the process in favor
of his kinsman. The Professor hails from the North,
being the same region as Muhammadu Buhari of the All
Progressive Congress (APC) who was Jonathan's major
opposition. As President Jonathan and his wife struggled with accreditation, General Buhari, and his wife,
Aisha Buhari, were accredited without any hitch in their
home town, Duara, Katsina.

President Jonathan, rather unwisely, totally failed to
read the handwritings on the wall about Professor Jega's
poor supervision and process unpreparedness. The President ignored Jega's suspicious partisan engagements,
lack of transparency, and his boldfaced ability to lie to
his country regarding the ballot process supervisory
readiness. He failed to learn from the history and reality

of his country's electoral process - that the sitting President reserves the absolute power over the head of the electoral sector, and could remove him for significant reasons. Yet Jega prevailed uninterrupted even when it was obvious that INEC had lost its credibility to deliver ballot fairness or credibility.

Another blunder that wrecked President Jonathan in his quest for a next tenure was the oversight of his campaign team. While the opposition, APC were ceaselessly overrunning the voting population with campaign propaganda, runners of President Jonathan's campaign were busy scrambling and garnering funds for their personal interests. Does it bother Jonathan that Colonel Sambo Dasuki, his former National Security Adviser allegedly diverted $2.1 billion meant for arms purchase for other unrelated matters? It was alleged that these funds were diverted into President Jonathan's presidential campaign coffer, though prevalent records show no such connections. Yet it is troubling that these fraudulent activities occurred undetected and unchecked right under Jonathan's watch.

In a post-election scrutiny of the current Nigerian political system, it must be noted that both the People's Democratic Party (PDP) and All Progressive Congress (APC) are still in denial about their roles and flaws in this past general election. Let the truth be told - that President Jonathan and his PDP handlers, unwisely stumbled, while General Buhari and his APC handlers deceitfully usurped victory. PDP claimed Jonathan stepped down out of humility to avoid an anticipated post-election violence, whereas APC branded Buhari a hero who won because Nigerians wanted a change of system. For the records, it must be noted that, letting 'him' have 'yours' out of ignorance is not humility, it is stupidity. Similarly, victory by deception doesn't make one a hero, but a rogue. Hence, there were no heroes in Nigeria's 2015 ballot calamity; neither were there any humble losers. However, there was a confused incumbent, surrounded by selfish handlers, who watched tactlessly while some inglorious rogues absconded with his throne in a typical "daylight snatch-and-grab" assault manner.

After any election, especially in a race as controversial as the PDP-APC presidential polls, a "postmortem" is compulsory. This enables the players explore relevant thoughts about their performances. Winners are engrossed in strategizing about implementing projections, whereas losers evaluate their losses to make amends. Hence, managing failure remains one of the best part of effective governance. In organizational leadership, failure is not unacceptable. What might be disastrous is when managers fail to immediately assess measures, and reconcile their lapses.

However, in the Nigerian system, the situation is absolutely the opposite. Most winners are immediately oc-cupied with infighting over their opportunities to loot public funds. Others winners are busy lampooning losers with foul language for losing. Losers on their own part, are enthralled in some "don't blame it on me" mentality.

Even before the presidential inauguration, some losers had already abandoned their political ideologies, "car-pet-crossing", to shower the winning Presidential candi-date with congratulatory messages in order to scheme for appointed positions. This is Nigeria - a system where the application of politics as a tool for national develop-ment lacks merit. In this system, politics is about re-sources sharing, geo-political zoning, power-grabbing and treasury looting – all at the expense of the poor and impoverished constituents.

Another devastating part of post-election party poli-tics is a campaign by President Jonathan's handlers, cat-egorizing him as a martyr and hero for accepting his disgraceful defeat. To make matters worse, President Jonathan absconded after his loss, leaving his party hopeless without leadership. This attitude reveals an-other side of his temperament; a lack of courage to reor-ganize his disciples and weather the political storm. Rather than reconvene to access and reconcile a cocktail of mistakes that precipitated and aggravated their fail-ure, the PDP went amok in the social media to glorify a leader who erred, lost, gave up, and ran off.

In the very conservative Nigeria's learning community, celebrating a self-inflicted failure is inconceivable. Why would anybody idolize a loser for doing just about what any loser would do - admit and accept his loss? For goodness sake, why would anyone glorify a captain who miscalculated, derailed, admitted failure, and abandoned his ship?

In the complex world of organizational leadership, rewarding excellence makes sense because it encourages a culture of hard work, perseverance, and operational efficacy. Rewarding excellent behaviors also create a functioning environment of ethical decency. President Jonathan was a good leader endowed with core transformational competencies that could have moved his country further to inseparable unity if he had triumphed for a second tenure. He must be acknowledged for humbly accepting his loss, but proclaiming him a hero in a race he disgracefully handled and fled, simply sends the wrong message about motivating success and managing excellence.

As stated earlier in this book, failure in transformation management is not a taboo but a challenge that could be managed through identifying and reconciling ambiguities; and resolving them strategically to create a better future. As entrepreneurship scholar, *Scott Shane* noted, people will not try to do new things if they know that they would be punished for failing. Thus, as a culture, tolerating failure, in fact, makes organizations more innovative and effective. Jonathan and PDP's disastrous election outing must not be outlawed as an incorrigible measure; neither must their failure be scorned as disgrace. Rather, the whole process must be recorded as a learning curve - a platform - to reorganize and move on. Nevertheless, to glorify this failure might translate to a scorn of excellence.

THE HOMECOMING

■ In his first 14 days in the job, he surprised the entire country with 14 exceptional executive tasks. He held five private meetings to get hold of the national security and intelligence; five secret meetings to initiate a transfer of the nation's armory to Borno State – his preferred location; one oversea trip, and three major shameful oratory blunders.

SEVEN
Homecoming of the Ruler

■ For a man, President Muhammadu Buhari, who
once led a coup that ended his country's path to a second republic; a man who once suspended the constitution and ruled as a despot, all that glittered might not
just be gold.

Before we get engaged with substantial issues of this
chapter, we must please note that;

■ Disapproval of Buhari's style of governance is
not an attack on the Northern Nigerians because
Buhari does not represent the North but himself,

his obscure mission, and his ancestral interests.

■ Discussion about Boko Haram is not an attack on Muslims because Boko does not represent Muslims but her own brutal sectarian interests.

■ Expressing concerns about Buhari's fight against corruption is not an attack on implanting moral decency in the system, but a condemnation of tyranny, discriminatory justice, (gagging of the Press), and suppression of the judicial process.

For a man, President Muhammadu Buhari, who once led a coup that ended his country's path to a second republic; a man who once suspended the constitution and ruled as a despot, all that glittered might not just be gold. Prior to his election, the All Progressive Congress (APC) had promised Nigerians that their candidate - an ex-dictator - had been intellectually refurbished to undertake the challenges of the representative system. However, barely 30 days after taking office, Nigerians became worried about their new leader and his single-handed approach to essential issues of governance.

Besides his inability to communicate guidelines, critics and observers were worried that President Buhari, who was yet to name a single minister or adviser months after his inauguration resumed duties unaccompanied; and randomly verbalized policies without applicable process, and without consideration of mandatory factors.

For instance, his directive to dissolve the board of the state oil company as an attempt to fight corruption in the industry was immediately faulted as redundant and con- stitutionally unnecessary. According to the "Petroleum Act," the board stood dissolved the moment erstwhile Petroleum Minister, Diezani Alison-Madueke, left of- fice. This served as an indication that President Buhari was not familiar with the rules of public engagement in a democracy.

Weeks after his inauguration, President Buhari, with- out consultation with the appropriate sectors, went on the air to declare that his country's treasury was "virtu- ally empty," claiming his predecessors had stolen bil- lions of dollars. But the immediate past minister of national planning, Dr Abubarka Sulaiman, quickly dep- recated these claims as inaccurate, expressing with phys- ical proofs, that the former regime left about $30 billion before handing over.

Similarly, Babs Omotowa, the chief executive of the Nigerian Liquefied Natural Gas Company (NLNG), claimed that the company paid $1.6 billion in dividends to the Buhari government, adding that the President was either hiding the correct amount paid to his government in order to justify his claim of inheriting "an empty treasury" or that the NLNG was playing a game on Nigerians.

The political climate soon degenerated to a chaotic atmosphere. A newly inaugurated Senate president, Dr. Bukola Saraki had opened up on plans made by un-named individuals to kidnap and prevent him from emerging the senate president. It may be recalled that President Buhari and his party members chose another candidate, Femi Gbajabiamila for this position. Dr. Saraki however, outmaneuvered their plans by arriving at the facility as early as 6am, and remained in premises till the resumption of house business. Hence, his emer-gence as the senate president came as a surprise to both President Buhari and his party.

Nigerians took to the social media, communicating threads of frustrations and expressions of disappoint-ment about the direction of the regime in bringing about a proposed transformation. Citizens, who at this time re-lied predominantly on ill-informed party bloggers to learn about important government policies, now ques-tioned a disconnection between their new leader and pertinent engagements of the representative process.

To make it worse, the newly inaugurated 8th National Assembly, expected to collaborate with the presidency on ministerial appointments, deliberated only on their huge allowances and adjourned for four weeks. The APC had initially claimed that Buhari was waiting on the National Assembly to convene so he could present his team but before the recess, ministerial appointments remained an obscure gamble. The Deputy Senate Presi-dent, Sen Ike Ekweremadu, in response to a public outcry twitted, "We will reconvene once the Ministerial list is ready." Internal party sources claimed that an in-house tussle between the President and party stalwarts over choice of ministerial positions grounded his appointments.

President Buhari soon sailed beyond his autocratic demeanor. His skills to undertake the new leadership challenges became another factor that further jeopardized his chances to succeed. For instance, in the first 14 days in the job, he surprised the entire country with 14 exceptional executive tasks. He held five private meetings to get hold of the national security and intelligence; five secret meetings to initiate a transfer of the nation's armory to Borno State – his preferred location; one oversea trip, and three major shameful oratory blunders. In several dishonorable speech miseries, he had referred to the German Chancellor, Angela Merkel as *President Michelle* and referred to Germany as *West Germany.*

Therefore, without doubt, Nigerians had every reason to worry about this leader. In a complex economy, installing a leader without relevant skills is like hiring a tailor to an Intensive Care Unit to perform surgery, just because they can handle needle and thread. A leader who swaggered the transformation mantra as an electioneering promise could at least deliver some basic skills such as; transparency with public issues, collaboration with subordinates, and funny enough, the ability to appropriately identify names of friendly countries, and their leaders.

It is one thing to rustle power and an entirely different thing to manage it. Truly, Buhari and APC, became confused about "change." They were subjugated by the demands of the transformation process which they themselves professed, and were, disgracefully, overwhelmed by their own campaign promises, regarding how and where to commence. Hence as a remedy, it must be noted that; in the world of executive governance, confusion is not a taboo but a challenge that can be managed through reconciling ambiguities, admitting to contradictions and resolving them, while still maintaining a functioning capacity. An existing incompatible Buhari/APC team cannot overcome this shortfall through their usual deception of the masses, playing hide-and-sick with critical issues of public policy, and engaging in fruitless media attack of a predecessor that had long gone.

EIGHT

Buhari wonders: Executive stalemate

■ Let us be clear then - because a president chose a wheelbarrow as an official car does not make him morally decent and fiscally astute; it only exposes his ignorance to fiscal policies and security issues.

Unable to choose his working team months after his swear-in, President Muhammadu Buhari struggled to kick-off a regime he bragged so much about. The All Progressives Congress, APC, it may be recalled, ran an electioneering race projecting their candidate as a fiscally astute conservative, who would curb corruption and appropriately manage the country's economic and financial resources. The masses got something entirely different.

While Buhari, a former dictator, struggled with official duties in a representative system unfamiliar to his individual aptitude, his camp was busy showcasing him with falsehood and deceptive fairy tales. To substitute for total lack of answers for his regime's catastrophe, the APC social media warriors fed disappointed masses with some worthless cock-and-bull tales of what was termed the "Buhari Wonders."

The first fake story to justify Buhari's humility, and considerateness to money matters came during the government transition period, when the APC claimed that predecessor, Dr. Goodluck Jonathan presented a billion Naira budget for delegates' lunch, but Buhari the "good money-manager" declined any expenses, saying that his transition team would bring their own lunch. Meanwhile this president was in London at the time, on a controversial mission not properly communicated to his constituents.

Yet, a similar story made it to the social media network from the Buhari's camp, on how, during the South Africa's trip, Buhari paid the hotel bills for his staff, and asked the rest of the entourage to pay their own bills. This was a president yet to name a single staff as at that date. The propaganda continued with another rumor, claiming that hundreds of politicians, including the Petroleum Minister, Alison-Madueke had returned billions of Dollars stolen from the government - because they were afraid of Buhari, the "respected honest money-keeper" and disciplinarian.

It was rather despicable that at that crucial time in the regime, the APC social media ensemble, (who at this time were running out of Buhari praise-worship songs) were busy telling self-indulgent stories including comparing Buhari and Jonathan's cars; use of presidential jets; Buhari's choice of transportation, and ostensibly his choice of "suya flavor". But how long would they continue to feed the masses with these tommyrots?

Consistently, and most irritably, the Buhari's camp in the social media would tag around senseless stories about Buhari; like claiming he was opting to fly economy class over first class; or choosing to ride the popular motorbike public transportation system known as *Okada over official convoy; or proposing to eat his meals, sitting on the floor instead of an official dining table; or heading to Alhaji Suya shack for his inauguration dinner rather than the traditional Aso-Rock, in-house executive banquet.

Major questions remained regarding; when Nigerians

---

*Okada: a motorbike taxi. The name was derived from Okada Air, a Nigerian local airline popular in the 80s.

would get substantial information about the running of the government; where were the 'missing Chibok girls'? Or when exactly the 'change' process would start? Where were the unemployment salaries? Where were Buhari's ministers? Who had been making all decisions at the time? Or a major issue about whether Nigeria was still running a democracy?

Indeed, Buhari and those who bejeweled him into his current executive predicament faced a more complicated political landscape. Even as Buhari announced as a ter-ror-defense strategy, a relocation of the country's armory to Borno State, the region remained under terrorist bom-bardment. In fact, a major suicide bombing, at a crowded fish market occurred right in the heart of north-eastern city of Maiduguri - the same region where the regime relocated its arsenal.

Let us be clear then - because a president chose a wheelbarrow as an official car does not make him morally decent and fiscally astute; it only exposes his ig-norance to fiscal policies and security issues. Buhari, and indeed his entire embarrassment of *Yahoo* drum-beaters, at the time, could be explaining their frame-works and preparedness to fiscal reformation. They could be telling Nigerians how the regime could sustain in the long run, the existing spending and tax policies without jeopardizing the country's creditworthiness, ob-ligations or projected expenses.

Without Ministers at the time; not a single known adviser, and without any working team besides obsequious cohorts who were worshiping him, President Buhari was already abusing his official democratic duties, making contradictory policy comments, dictating unmanageable strategy undertakings, and flip-flopping with dire issues of national significance.

Urgently, the masses were waiting for their new president to at least acquaint them with his plans to proceed. They wanted to hear about the machinery to translate electoral promises into action, not about limousines, and jets. In a government structure where the President could not communicate, could not relate, and worse, could not corroborate his own policies, there was every reason to worry. It was torturing that under this regime, citizens had to rely on recalcitrant party bloggers to know the fate of their current economic woes.

Money-saving transportation convoy. **A s**atirical photo published in the
International Guardian about Buhari's official transportation convoy, lampooning   the APC social media warriors who fed disappointed masses with
some worthless cock-and-bull tales of what was termed the 'Buhari Wonders."

Consistently, and most irritably, the Buhari's camp in the social media would
tag around senseless stories about Buhari; like claiming he was opting to fly
economy class over first class; or choosing to ride the popular motorbike
public transportation system known as *Okada* over official convoy; or proposing to eat his meals, sitting on the floor instead of an official dining table;
or heading to Alhaji Suya shack for his inauguration dinner rather than the
traditional Aso-Rock, in-house, executive banquet.

NINE

Angry President, miserable nation

◼ Nigeria would disappointedly realize that cruelty to issues of governance does not stop terrorism, and cannot create any apparatus for unity – rather, it would rip this country further apart.

With poor documentaries apparently triggered by short memories over Nigeria's past political issues, the local and world's media apparently failed to understand that President Buhari walked into his current office very angry. The former dictator was bitter about several issues which he had vowed to address revengefully if he ever delved into the corridors of power, and surprisingly, he attained that opportunity.

Among other grievances, President Buhari had complained bitterly about the treatment of his tribesmen, the Fulani herdsmen by other communities; and he had condemned the categorization of Boko Haramn as a terrorist group. Branding these killers as his "misguided brothers", he had vowed to negotiate with them toward an unconditional amnesty; also, he had vowed to take revenge against career politicians and public officers instrumental in any manner, to his removal as a dictator in 1985; he was so upset about the decentralization of Nigeria's armory and had wanted it relocated to the North, to accord this region a greater command of the coercive power of governance if the need ever arose; furthermore, he had been bitter over the decentralization of the oil sector and had sworn to punish those who stood up to the system to wield the control away from the cartels.

In shear execution of his animosity, President Buhari had clamped down on the national security adviser, Sambo Dasuki, with charges of illegally possessing weapons. Dasuki's properties were raided and firearms were seized, while events of his arraignment were shared in the social media by agents of the President. Dasuki, it may be recalled, was among the coup plotters who dethroned Buhari after almost two years of his dictatorship (1983 –1985). Buhari was reportedly arrested by Dasuki on the eve of Sallah in 1985: and to dramatize his payback, on the same eve of Sallah in 2015, the angry and vindictive, democratically elected President Buhari, mischievously ordered the arrest of Dasuki with allegations of corruption and looting of public treasury.

As part of his payback scheme, President Buhari went after the Senate President, Dr. Bukola Saraki, orchestrated his arrest and prosecution on corruption through the Code of Conduct Tribunal (CCT), the Inspector General of Police, and the Justice Ministry. Saraki was slapped with a 13-count criminal charge by the Federal Ministry of Justice, and was subjected to social media character assassination campaign by paid agents of Buhari and his party, the All Progressive Congress (APC). But with their shortsightedness to issues of the past, Nigerians and indeed their various media outlets, regretfully, forgot why Buhari was picking on this man.

Senate President, Saraki, was in fact the son of the Late Chief Dr Olusola Saraki, a one-time Senate leader in the 2nd Republic (1979-1983) and a Senate committee member who indicted Buhari over a missing $2.8 billion stolen under his (Buhari's) watch as the Nigerian National Petroleum Corporation (NNPC) boss between 1977 and 1978. President Buhari was then indicted by the Nigerian Senate over the missing funds. The major reason being that, the money was traced to Buhari's bank accounts with a British bank, the Midland Bank, now HSBC. When Buhari and his military gangs took over power in 1983 through a coup, the late Senator Saraki was thrown behind bars together with members of his committee. The $2.8 Billion probe was then swept under the rug while all interconnected documents were destroyed by Buhari's Military Government.

Therefore, the regime's offensive against the current Senate President was a continuation of Buhari's avowed vendetta to destroy those he bitterly considered his political foes, and others he spitefully despises. Yet, it appeared the angry President was not done. Since his inauguration, he rallied his pay-back machinery against those who ran the oil sector for meddling with the status quo - a structure that, erstwhile, had given the North upper hands in affairs of oil and gas. He then accorded a few individuals from the North the control of the dividend, including blocks and service contracts. At the period, the Buhari (public misinformation) warriors took to the social media to celebrate the arrest of a former Petroleum Minister, Diezani Alison-Madueke, in London over Buhari's aggravated allegations of corruption and money laundering. When Nigerians who are loyal to Buhari's punitive agenda were busy celebrating, others concluded that this was a retaliatory push by the incoming administration against a minority - a woman for that matter - who stood up to the cartels that had always monopolized the petroleum sector.

Fighting corruption in a country where deceit in the structure is phenomenal; unquestionably defensible, but using this as a tactic to profile specific individuals might be repressive. For instance, President Buhari received valid documents and complete information about how the former governor of Rivers State, Chibuike Rotimi Amaechi who headed his campaign financed his Presidential race with embezzled funds. Unfortunately, Amaechi, together with other fraudulent politicians not only made it to President Buhari's ministerial list, but also trotted the world with him in some pricey trips that yielded nothing but more terrorist attacks, fiscal misery, and global humiliation. Yet Nigerians, even as their country creeped into depression and anarchy, were busy jubilating over Buhari's vindictive temperament – tyrannizing former public servants he had vowed to destroy so as to settle past scores.

For even at this time, Nigerians must be reminded that their president is angry and needs their prayers. Cheering a dictator clueless about issues of governance, but who is uncontrollably on rampage, flunking every rule of the democratic process, would be self-destructive. They ought to have seen this movie before, when Buhari ruled as a dictator. At some point, those Nigerians intoxicated by the regime's aimless "change" song; those folks who are now celebrating repression and hailing their dictator as he brutalizes others, would soon become major victims of this same policy they are endorsing. Sooner or later, Nigerians would also realize that jailing political foes in pretext of fighting corruption neither create jobs, nor grow the economy. They would disappointedly realize that cruelty to issues of governance does not stop terrorism, and cannot create any apparatus for unity – rather, it would rip this country further apart.

TEN

100 days of horror

■ In less than a hundred days, Buhari had thrown the country's economy into harm's way, singlehandedly presiding over changes that signaled a fiscal doom. He had enforced a mass worker retrenchment, sending close to 100,000 out of jobs.

It is one thing is to rustle power, but sustaining the challenges require more competencies. Nigerians debated the 100-day season of their new regime with critics bashing the presidency for leading a very sluggish start, while supporters of President Muhammadu Buhari declined to substantially defend his proposals. It could rightly be argued that the First 100 Days have never guaranteed the success of an entire tenure; neither have early process complications necessitated failure in governance. However, every voyage starts with one step (thanks to *Franklin D. Roosevelt,* a United States President), who in 1933, used his first three months in office to consolidate the foundations of his executive mandate. Ever since that year, the First 100 Days have been seen as a unique moment in predicting proposal efficacy and tenure effectiveness.

President Buhari's regime was still confused about governance, and at the worst, waterlogged by the demands of a transformation process it professed. Supported by his ruling party, President Buhari in his first 100 days was terribly astounded by his own campaign proposals – grappling with how and where to start, and openly denying the very promises he made to the masses just a few months prior.

A hundred days or not, the troubling issue was that President Buhari's accomplishments at the 100-day period were a horrendous nightmare. The President autocratically handled leadership in his own way without following any known leadership or project management praxis. In an authoritarian manner, constitutional measures were swiftly dwindling into unrestrained anarchy. In global political news and issues, Nigeria stood out, at the time, as the only country where an elected President ferociously assumed the positions of the vice president, chief prosecutor, prison director, chief judge, petroleum chief – then sits down on the constitution with unrestrained supremacy, cold-shouldering the other arms of government.

From the very start of his executive directives, President Buhari tackled the most significant issues in the country's politics – security, economy, and corruption. Regrettably, an observation of his handling of these, indicated that the country was once again, back to dictatorship. For instance, on security, he had quickly replaced the service chiefs; moved Nigeria's defense command unit to Maiduguri, claiming that the idea was to ease up a counter strategy against Haram terror group. His critics, however, differed, accusing Buhari of conferring greater political power opportunities to his Northern allies, and restructuring the military system to protect the "Northern Power" structure.

To further frustrate a global support of the fight against the Boko Haram terrorists, the Buhari regime was scandalously exposed for secretly granting an entry visa to a fleeing 'ISIS Emir', and a Lebanese fugitive, Ahmad al-Assir who was later arrested. He was trying to escape to Nigeria through Cairo with fake Palestinian travel document in a scenario that questions the Buhari's credibility in fighting terror. While a possible collaboration between Assir and the Buhari's regime was being investigated, Buhari's advocacy for a Boko Haram amnesty created additional doubts over his request for assistance from the United States in fighting terror, leaving the regime all confused and helpless in meeting its security proposals to defend the country.

In less than a hundred days, Buhari had thrown the country's economy into harm's way, singlehandedly presiding changes that signaled a fiscal doom. He had enforced a mass worker retrenchment, sending close to 100,000 out of jobs. He had banned the recruitment of federal public sector workers, raised interest rates, and halted capital projects at all governmental levels. Without any official protocol, he had dictatorially suspended the upgrade of projects at the Calabar/Onne seaports, ordered a slash in federal allocation to states, and canceled the second Niger Bridge project, attributing his actions to one single phrase, "war against corruption."

In less than three months after taking office, foreign investors and major global financial institutions openly expressed concerns about the direction of the Nigerian economy. In the same period, J.P. Morgan Chase & Co. disqualified Nigeria from its local-currency emerging-market bond indexes, after restrictions on foreign-exchange transactions prompted investor concerns about a shortage of liquidity. But, the defiant president remained untouched about his belt-tightening policy, and in fact announced a proposal to shut down some embassies and foreign missions abroad – another action that could put additional thousands of federal employees out of their jobs by last quarter of the year.

Just like his handle of the economy and matters of security, the regime's vows to tackle corruption remain another shocking blow. In sheer irony, Buhari was personally caught up reconciling issues of fraud directly involving his own interests. For instance, the immediate former governor of the oil rich Rivers State, Chibuike Rotimi Amaechi was at the time facing accusations of funding Buhari's Campaign with stolen state funds amounting to more than 70 billion Naira. Amaechi allegedly, fraudulently, sold state-owned power plants and made mistrustful transfer of $105 million (N21, 000,000,000) from the Power Asset Sale Proceeds Account to accounts owned by different private companies.

Consequently, the General was alleged to have personally pleaded with former President Chief Olusegun Obasanjo, one of the targets of his proposed probe, who had vowed to release a dossier of documents linking him (Buhari), his wife, daughter, and key allies in his administration, to major fraud related to various affairs of the past regimes. To appease the aged former leader, President Buhari quickly retracted his threats, announcing publicly that he would not extend his corruption probe beyond the administration of former President Goodluck

Jonathan.

One year after his inauguration as president, Buhari's drive to curb fraud yielded nothing besides indiscriminate arrests of selected individuals whom he had targeted for retributive reasons. As it has been clarified earlier in this book, criticisms of Buhari's fight against corruption is not an attack on implanting moral decency in the system, but a condemnation of tyranny, discriminatory justice, and suppression of the judicial process.

While this president, a former dictator, flip-flopped with official duties in a representative system unfamiliar to his individual capacity, his appointed media activists were busy showcasing him with falsehood and deception. To substitute for a total lack of responses for his regime catastrophe, the media combatants polluted the social media with fake stories about the Buhari's accomplishments. Yet, the regime's major damage remained Buhari's total disconnection with both his subordinates in the government, party colleagues, and the masses. In his signature tyrannical fashion, Buhari remained the only arm of the system, whereas his supporters chokingly struggled in the social media defending the vagueness of his stewardship. Shamelessly, the "Sai-Buhari" profile-glorification jingle totally expired into obscurity, leaving his media handlers redundant and clueless about their ostracized approach in defending mediocrity.

ELEVEN

Abuse and crash of the "Change" praxis

■ Besides a routine abuse of the change practice since his inauguration, the President may have finally crashed what was left of his credibility to fight moral laxity, and the ability to execute a transformation process he professed and paraded as his supervisory forte.

SOCIAL media discussion threads were swamped with debates about Nigeria, and a controversy about the list of ministerial nominees made public by its president, Muhammadu Buhari. Majority of the masses almost running out of patience, had waited for almost four months for their new leader to announce his ministerial team, and had equally criticized him for sluggishly sitting down on many issues of national significance. But the Presidency explicitly defended his delays of ministerial nominations, claiming it needed enough time to search for credible people to harmonize with his professed transformation agenda. He had, uncontrollably, used the term "change" to pacify their justified impatience.

The nation was shocked when the list of ministerial nominees was finally released and sent to the Senate by the Presidency for endorsement. Disgracefully, most nominees turned out to be the same politicians and public officers with accusations of embezzlement, mismanagement, and corruption blurring their records. The issues on political dynamics thus took a new turn, revealing that the President may have misled the nation when he claimed he was taking his time to search for honest and capable hands.

Another issue provoked by the President's list centers on the "Change" philosophy affirmed by the President and his party, the All Progressive Congress (APC) as their governance approach. As a campaign strategy, Buhari's camp had adopted the change mantra as an anthem, wooing their base with chocolate-coated transformation lyrics, and singing themselves into power. But besides a routine abuse of the practice since his inauguration, the President may have finally crashed what was left of his credibility to fight moral laxity, and the ability to execute a transformation process he professed and paraded as his supervisory forte.

President Buhari's handle of the country at the time - almost four months into his assumption of power, convinced Nigerians across party lines that the regime had no idea about what to do with power in a representative process. It was unfortunate that the regime had no blueprint to move the country forward, but were trapped with a President who neither communicated nor collaborated with subordinates but woke up daily, with strange attitude, disagreeing with himself, and pronouncing tactless orders.

Most Nigerians, without doubt were convinced then that the regime had battled unproductively with the perception of the change praxis. Yet, failure in any leadership process, could not have be treated as a forbidden concept but as a learning ground to make amends and proceed. Pronouncing change as a theme could be one thing, but understanding and executing the technicalities require a more thinking approach. Below are a few summaries about the reality of the practice of the change discipline;

■ The first determinant of 'change' as a solution is the quality of the proposed transformation. A proposal to fight corruption with corrupt characters is not change, but reveals a total bastardization of the "process of change". In the realm of ethical management, it takes moral people to shape a moral society. The names and characters in Buhari's list did not correspond with that philosophy.

■ Change does not mean a rearrangement of managers and positions; it is not about firing workers for poor performance or jailing jobless youth for shop-lifting. Change is a science – an embrace of a new paradigm strategically executed to inspire a solid foundation for future developments.

■ A quest for organizational renewal requires a constructive blueprint. A Change expedition without a plan is like flying a passenger jet without a satellite-based navigation system. Since its inauguration, Buhari's regime has not presented any development outline, while the president, had consistently, singlehandedly made decisions in a dictatorial manner. In a structure supervised by a team of politicians unfamiliar with the dialect of change, the masses must be ready for further surprises.

■ In the complex world of political governance, change does not mean a change of address from Daura to Abuja. It is obvious that the regime does not understand the political meaning of "Change", but has unwisely shown a biased movement, recycle, and reshuffle of people, positions, and the national resources. This is not "change", but a systematized smash-and-grab invasion of the nation, its people, resources, and prospects.

12

TWELVE
Appointees and
diversity management

■ In any transformation process, diversity in workforce is an ethical mandate not a treat.

Nigerians boiled in controversy over their new
leader's approach to appointment of ministers and other
governmental positions. President Muhammadu Buhari,
almost 100 days in office then, had appointed mostly in-
digenes of the North, where he hails from, to occupy
key positions in his regime, in a manner that generated a
widespread uproar, with critics labelling his actions as

"lopsided."

From many threads that pervade the social media about this issue, one commentator wrote, "No Southerner is looking for handouts from their Southern representatives, rather we simply want all parts of the whole to be equally represented." Another individual identified as a retired police commissioner echoed a similar sentiment labelling the appointments as unequal, saying, "Nigeria is too big to have majority of the appointees from one section of the country. We have competent people in every part of Nigeria. For that reason, Buhari should spread the appointments to every part of Nigeria."

Most of Buhari's supporters, however saw nothing wrong with his appointments, arguing that choosing a team of his choice is a part his executive mandate. In fact, one member of his party told the media that Buhari's appointments were "wonderful and forward looking." He said, "There is nothing wrong with it because the leader wants to put people who are going to help achieve the promise they made to the people." To further support the President's actions, a news blog, *Delta Analyst Online* reported on how a pastor in the city of Benin backed the President's actions saying, "If Buhari appoints a 'monkey' as one of those to assist him to bring the change he has promised, Nigerians should support him".

But Buhari's actions should have been expected based on his own comments less than six weeks prior. In a forum in his visit to the United State, President Buhari had categorically stated that he would not treat people who did not vote for him equally with those who voted for him. In his words, the President had stated, "Going by election results, constituencies that gave me 97% cannot in all honesty be treated, on some issues, (the same way) with constituencies that gave me 5%. I think these are political realities."

Thus Buhari's latest disregard of issues of equity and fairness in his allotment of crucial executive positions came, not as a surprise, rather a practical execution a proposal he had already put in place. Attorney and legal analyst, Oshiokpekhai Utu-Orbih cited possible constitutional lapses of Buhari's appointment as "a total disregard for due process of law and order," citing Section 14 (3) of the Nigerian 1999 Constitution mandating equity in composition of national government. Utu-Orbih denounced Buhari's appointments as a scheme running contrary to the spirit and letters of this constitutional provision, and argued that Buhari's onslaught on the Nigerian people has surely awakened a new consciousness that could inspire a unity of the Southerners as formidable oppositions.

It may be necessary however, to view President Buhari's disproportionate executive appointment at the time from other perspectives. Besides the provisions of the laws, balancing the workforce in a diverse culture is not just an administrative requirement, but an ethical duty. An uneven work structure amorally leaves an unproductive environment of dichotomy and a marginalized populace. Constitution or not, it is ethically erroneous (in a population diverse with multiple tribes, cultures, and geographical sectors), to ostracize any group from the leadership or the workforce process.

Demographic trends in contemporary governance leaves three interrelated leadership challenges; cross-cultural complexities, gender disparities, and diversity management. Without doubt, President Buhari, so far, has failed to recognize the inevitability of these concepts in his stewardship, and repercussions may derail his push for a transformation.

There are various studies to substantiate the powerful effects of workforce evenness in decision-making effectiveness. Hence, to progress in his vows to effectively transform his country, President Buhari could embrace a plan that would encompass a judicious composition of the people and relevant demographic arrangements, including; culture, tribes, gender, and geopolitical zones.

In transformation management, especially in a multicultural society, diversity in governmental appointees is a moral mandate not a treat. Using appointment of key public positions to reward campaign supporters, support tribesmen, or punish those considered as "unsupportive" constituents are ethically unjust, spiteful, and may not create the necessary avenues to inspire change.

Furthermore, Buhari's cohorts could have enlightened him on issues of diversity regarding public policy, rather than their current self-justifying mentality. A consideration of gender, tribe, age, and geopolitical zones must play a role in structuring the executive workforce to inspire any growth. The electorates or followers, who are indeed a core segment of the democratic process, are humans who have emotional and psychological needs, and compromising those needs could create resentment and resistance to any transformation agenda. The regime, visibly, has already been experiencing such resentments.

The electorates or followers, who are indeed a core segment of the democratic process, are humans who have emotional and psychological needs, and compromising those needs could create resentment and resistance to any transformation agenda. The regime, visibly, has already been experiencing such resentments. Here is an eastern-based group, the Indigenous People of Biafra on a peaceful protest against the regime on Ikwerre Road, Port Harcourt.

Photo: International Guardian/Archives.

13

THIRTEEN

How does a 50% pay cut crack terror?

■ The beleaguered masses were saturated with
pointless campaigns regarding Buhari's holier-than-
thou personality. This would have been the time to
show his executive skills and thus far, he flunked that
test.

Few months into his regime, Boko Haram militants
had slaughtered villagers and bombed churches and
mosques in Northern Nigeria within few weeks, thus
challenging President Muhammadu Buhari's vows to
clean the region of any terrorist insurgency in the first

few months of his administration. To make it worse, the group had boldly overrun Borno State, a region where President Buhari relocated the country's armory, with an excuse to defeat them. So what went wrong?

A week prior, frustrated Nigerians took to media outlets to question President Buhari's nonchalant attitude toward issues of security and economy. He had remained out of touch with realities of the governmental process, and had not offered a single plan as to how to begin. Food prices were on the increase; Fuel pump price had multiplied in geometrical figures. Foreign exchange figures was on a scary increase, contrary to Buhari's promise to eliminate differences in rates.

Amidst all these difficulties and of course, the regime's inability to communicate a development outline, the president finally broke his 40-day silence on national issues. It was an announcement meant to positively inspire hope in a system currently lifeless. To his hopeless suffering masses, President Buhari handed down his announcement, that he would only receive half of the salary paid to his predecessor. Who cares? The annual salary of the Nigerian president is currently set at 14,058,820 Naira ($70,000), including allowances. The commonsense question was how a voluntary pay cut by this president could alleviate the current economic woes for the suffering masses?

Yet it was worrisome that, rather than tackle major issues, the social media warriors of the All Progressive Congress (APC) had continued to feed disappointed masses with worthless cock-and-bull tales about President Buhari's acclaimed modesty, cheap maintenance, and low-level lifestyle. Press releases were issued on either how he turned down an official car, or how he flew the economy class.

But observers remained very worried about this self-gratifying campaign. In a region overrun by Islamic extremists and terrorists, the major issue could not have been how a 50% pay-cut could crack terror. Buhari's supporters claim that his pay-cut would, likely, put pressure on members of the parliament and state governors to do the same, but how this attitude addressed skyrocketing unemployment rates was yet to be ascertained. Furthermore, with continual global slump in the price of crude oil, which was Nigeria's major source of revenue, the government was unable to disclose a figurative analysis on how pay-cuts could build the economy.

Challenges in government are inevitable: addressing them should be a strategic duty, not a punitive labor. One positive aspect of failure is that success thrives on it. Every country has that moment in time - a period when challenges engulf growth and possibilities. This is when policy-making effectiveness becomes obligatory, and the chief executive takes the lead in coordinating two significant elements of his duties, the general masses and the surrounding situation or context. A leader who neither understands nor speaks this language ought to step back and become a follower.

When president Obama came into office in 2008, the economy of the United States was in shambles. He named his team, presented America with a blue print, and communicated projected timelines. He spoke to the masses regularly through radio/TV speeches, social media chats, emails, and other outlets, expressing the desolations of the tide and his keenness to inspire change and convey hope into the populace. In January 2009 alone, employers cut nearly 800,000 workers. Throughout 2009, the job slashing continued until the unemployment rate hit 10 percent that October. Within four years, the unemployment rate went down to 5.6 percent, and at some point, the private-sector employers added jobs for 58 straight months — the longest streak on record.

One of President Obama's economic nightmares, inherited from his predecessor, was the housing catastrophe. The brutal foreclosure crisis knocked millions out of their homes, and by 2010, the "serious" delinquency rate for mortgages hit 4.2 percent, leaving millions of homeowners behind on their payments. Following Obama's blueprint, the delinquency rate was down to 1.9 percent while the housing prices rebounded.

Back to Nigeria and the prevalent standoff between

the administration and the masses on policymaking a
blackout, it must be known that nobody had expected a
miracle from this regime, but with its customary lack of
communication regarding projects' plans and timelines,
the Buhari's regime might be headed for a process
blackout. He was already abusing his official duties,
making contradictory policy comments, dictating unmanageable strategy undertakings, and flip-flopping
with dire issues of national significance.

For instance, without senate approval President
Buhari had unilaterally granted over N780 billion to
States without a signed document from an operational
minister of finance. While the APC bragged about the
president turning down official cars and presidential jets,
Buhari had unilaterally approved, and had started a con-
struction of a private helipad in Daura Katsina State, his
home town.

Electioneering campaign had been over, and by now,
the APC should have abstained from feeding hungry
masses with fake rhetoric and deceits about President
Buhari's sanctimonious lifestyle. It is not late for this
President to communicate his agenda and acquaint the
populace with his plans to proceed. Self-gratifying tales
about taking pay cuts, turning down official cars, declin-
ing state dinner engagements, and so on are absolutely
irrelevant to the current challenges. The poor masses
have long been saturated with pointless campaigns on

Buhari's holier-than-thou personality. This was the time to show his executive skills and so far, he had flunked that test.

FOURTEEN
The "Sai" Mentality

■ The "Sai mentality" also avowed a brainless prehistoric mindset that might have been soaked in deceit, misinformation, and fraud, but yielded no
substantial answer to practical issues of the regime's
current governance predicament.

The All Progressive Party (APC), under which platform President Buhari came into office, ran his campaign under a slogan "Sai Buhari." "Sai" is a Hausa term
that usually could be used for words or phrases such as
"until, not until, then, except, no one except." The APC

campaign slogan, "Sai Buhari" literally means that no one else is worthy or capable except Buhari.

Promotion with this slogan soon gathered necessary steam and ignited the electoral base. The APC took advantage and flooded the network with inconceivable electioneering promises – adopting this slogan as the answer and solution to virtually every question or concern regarding their manifestoes. Also, "Sai Buhari" fitted perfectly into the political terrain, especially in a race that came down to a two-man fistfight between Buhari and the then incumbent, Goodluck Jonathan, the flag-bearer for the People's Democratic Party.

As a slogan, "Sai Buhari" stood out as a powerful campaign catchphrase, and penetrated the constituents like wildfire, overwhelming billboards, and suffusing the social media in various presentational formats. However, the execution of the campaign promises that trailed the "Sai Buhari" strategy was utterly disregarded and could not offer voters the needed hope. For instance, one year after President Buhari's inauguration as president, virtually all the "Sai Buhari" campaign promises were grounded in obscurity, while he struggled with every segment of his official obligation, from economy, social, cultural, through core issues of constitutional commitment.

The APC also used this slogan as a cover-up, to protect the scrutiny of a candidate who might have been incompetent; had no relevant vision, mission, or passion for a position he contested. Blunders made by President Buhari before and shortly after his inauguration were a substantiation that Nigeria masses may have made a wrong choice, settling for a leader unfamiliar with the language and culture of contemporary governance.

For instance; during a heated campaign period in Owerri, the Imo state capital, as the APC presidential candidate, Buhari failed to recollect the name of his running mate, Yemi Osibanjo, and disgracefully called him "Yemi Osinbade." The video went viral with the opposition questioning his conceptual capacity to spontaneously articulate and relate issues.

The situation got worse even after his inauguration, when the Chief Executive trotted the globe unleashing shameful oratory blunders from one country to the other. In his trip to the United States, one of his major diplomatic outings after his inauguration, May 29, 2015, while speaking with his host, President Obama about the peaceful power transition in Nigeria, he had referred to his party, the All Progressive Congress to as "All Nigeria's People's Congress." In another trip to Germany, President Buhari before a foreign media panel had referred to Germany as "West Germany" – when historically, West Germany seized to exist since 1990. In the same speech, he referred to the Chancellor of Germany Angela Merkel as "President Michelle of West Germany".

Whereas observers expressed mixed reactions about these gaffes and other missteps that heralded the initial moments of his presidency, the negative consequences remain factual, that this President may have delved into an executive suit beyond his intellectual capacity. Every evidence points to the fact that he had no straightforward mission. His words and actions were also a substantiation of policy-making ambiguity. For instance, in his visit to Benin Republic where he met a group of resident Nigerian community members, the President yet spoke another blunder that left his constituents confused about their new leader. Reacting to a question on what his administration was doing to facilitate their return home, Buhari charged his country folks in the Diaspora to remain in the foreign land because he would not want them to add to the problem of unemployment back home. Here were his words in part:

> "I believe a lot of you are doing well and are better off here. So, the question of facilitating you to come home does not arise… We don't want you to come back home and be unemployed. Don't come and add to our problems…. If you have something doing here please, continue doing it."

Today, after one year of his executive mandate, Nigeria's issues have dwindled to the worst in a situation that left observers and analysts speechless. As mentioned earlier in this book, in a complex economy, installing a leader without relevant skills is like hiring a tailor in an Intensive Care Unit to perform surgery just because he can use a scissors, needle and thread.

Confusion management is critical to confronting challenges in any transformation process, but a constructive strategy has to be in place. One year into his four-year projected tenure, Buhari and the APC are still dazed and confused about "change"; they are subjugated by the demands of a transformation process they professed; and they are appallingly overwhelmed by their own campaign promises with little or no clue about how and where to start.

As a remedy, it may be noted that; in the world of executive governance, confusion is not a curse word but a challenge that can be managed through reconciling ambiguities, admitting to contradictions, and resolving them while still maintaining a functioning capacity. Yet an existing incompatible Buhari/APC brotherhood cannot overcome this shortfall through their current deception of the masses, playing hide-and-sick with critical issues of public policy, and fruitless media attack on a predecessor that had long gone.

The "Sai Buhari" slogan flourished as a ploy to escape thousands of basic electioneering questions awaiting President Buhari and APC about their incredible promises. The slogan ended up as a hopeless chant that

Then APC candidate, **Buhari** *demonstrates the "Sai Buhari" jingle.* The slogan stood out as a powerful campaign catchphrase, and penetrated the constituents like wildfire, overwhelming billboards, and suffusing the social media in various presentational formats. However, the execution of the campaign promises that trailed the "Sai Buhari" strategy was utterly disregarded and could not offer voters the needed hope. For instance, one year after President Buhari's inauguration as president, virtually all the "Sai Buhari" campaign promises remained in obscurity, while he struggled with every segment of his official obligation, from economy, social, cultural, through core issues of constitutional commitment.

Photo: International Guardian/Archives.

bears no relevance to the President's ability and readiness to lead a complex economy. The "Sai mentality" also avowed a brainless prehistoric mindset that might have been soaked in deceit, misinformation, and fraud, but yielded no substantial answer to practical issues of the regime's current governance predicament.

FINAL THOUGHTS

■ As mentioned earlier in this book, organizational change is not a reshuffle of employees and position; neither is it a mass retrenchment of the workforce to complement the dryness of the treasury. It is a strategic process designed to move the country from the present to a projected future state of economic possibilities and success. This process works faster with an innovative leader who has the vision to progress.

15

FIFTEEN

Buhari: In his own words

■ In the heat of his electioneering campaign, Feb 26 2015, President Buhari had stormed the *Chatham House* in London to market his presidential aspirations. He made sense of his topic, but within the lines, he made several vows which he currently flunks.

Good leaders inspire trust by communicating clear principles and maintaining a high level of personal integrity. Apart from making lengthy electioneering promises, leadership effectiveness demands inspiring cognitive strategies to transform plans into action. It could also necessitate self-evaluation of competencies where threats and weaknesses are transformed into a fruitful ground of opportunities. Has President Buhari lived through these values?

Judging from the last three major speeches* made by President Buhari, it is obvious that Nigeria may have been courted a leader who may not be trusted with his words. These three significant speeches – one in his electioneering campaign, second as an acceptance remarks of his election victory, and the third, his inaugural speech as the president – may have been riddled with contradictions, inconsistencies, and deceit.

In the heat of his electioneering campaign, Feb 26 2015, President Buhari had stormed the Chatham House, an independent policy institute, based in London to market his presidential aspirations. He made sense of his topic, *"Prospects for Democratic Consolidation in Africa: Nigeria's Transition",* but within the lines, he made several vows which he currently flunks. For instance, he emphasized that any war waged on corruption should not be misread as settling old scores or a witch-hunt, stating "I'm running for President to lead Nigeria to prosperity and not adversity."

What has become rather apparent, however, is his current vindictive approach in fighting graft. This President

---

*See Buhari's Speeches; *Chatham House Speech (Page 105); Acceptance Speech (Page 117), and his Inaugural Speech (125).*

would be deceiving the populace if he still maintains that he is not hiding under this "War Against Corruption" to settle past scores. I have in this book indicated how Buhari had clamped down on the former National Security Adviser, Sambo Dasuki, with charges of illegally possessing weapons. Dasuki was one of the coup plotters who dethroned Buhari after almost two years of his dictatorship (1983-1985). Buhari was, reportedly, arrested by Dasuki on the eve of Sallah in 1985. In a tit-for-tat manner, Buhari instructed the arrest of Dasuki on the eve of Sallah 2015., and ensured his public castigation and humiliation, in a "trial-by-media" format.

I also indicated how, as part of his payback scheme, President Buhari went after the Senate President, Dr. Bukola Saraki, orchestrated his arrest and prosecution on charges of corruption. Senate President, Saraki, is in fact, the son of the late Chief Dr Olusola Saraki, a one-time Senate leader in the 2nd Republic (1979-1983). The late Saraki was the Senate committee member who indicted Buhari, at the time, over a missing $2.8 billion which was said to have been stolen under Buhari's watch as the then boss of the Nigerian National Petroleum Corporation (NNPC), between 1977 and 1978. These and a thread of other punitive measures against those who are perceived to have "wronged" this President are, in fact, outrightly vindictive.

April 1st, 2015, Buhari now a President-elect, made

an acceptance speech after his election victory where he continued with his inconceivable agenda. The most observable fact about President Buhari's remarks is that he doesn't seem to understand his own assertions. Here was the President elect;

> "I pledge myself and the government to the rule of law, in which none shall be so above the law that they are not subject to its dictates, and none shall be so below it that they are not availed of its protection."

Buhari's pledge to adhere to his country's rule of law continued. In his inaugural speech on May 29, 2015, he affirmed his support for the judiciary, and other arms of government, stating;

> "It is only when the three arms act constitutionally that government will be enabled to serve the country optimally and avoid the confusion all too often bedeviling governance today."

Most disappointedly, in less than six months after theses pledges, President Buhari was already bullying the legislative and judicial arms, performing the duties of the Attorney General and Minister of Justice – with all judges reporting to him, and all court rulings or judgements screened before delivery. So how could this President fight corruption when he is abusing the judicial arm, violating court orders, and terrorizing judges?

In the most deceptive comment in his inaugural

speech, President Buhari had denounced the Boko Haram terrorists, describing them as "mindless, godless group who are as far away from Islam as one can think of." In addition, he vowed that his government will do all it can to rescue alive, 276 girls seized two years ago, by the Islamic extremists.

While the country was still angry over lack of progress to resolve this kidnappings, the Buhari regime had already announced an amnesty for the terror group's members who would turn themselves in. To make it worse, the regime established a camp to rehabilitate and reintegrate members of the killer-group who would surrender and would express remorse for their actions.

An estimated 20,000 people have been killed since Boko Haram began its campaign of violence in 2009. To substitute for this carnage, the Buhari regime believes that a verbal expression of remorse by some deadly terrorists still ruling his northern region with suicide bombings and foreign mercenaries was appropriate.

President Buhari's approach could exceed the conventional perception of authority, and implant some human qualities. Rather than his current projected or preferred status as a Roman god, he could develop an impeccable leader-follower relationship by simply communicating the truth to strategically open up constructive dialogue, and create listening opportunities to better serve his constituents.

Prospects for Democratic Consolidation
in Africa: Nigeria's Transition

"Permit me to start by thanking Chatham House for the invitation to talk about this important topic at this crucial time. When speaking about Nigeria overseas, I normally prefer to be my country's public relations and marketing officer, extolling her virtues and hoping to attract investments and tourists. But as we all know, Nigeria is now battling with many challenges, and if I refer to them, I do so only to impress on our friends in the United Kingdom that we are quite aware of our shortcomings and are doing our best to address them.

The 2015 general election in Nigeria is generating a lot of interests within and outside the country. This is understandable. Nigeria, Africa's most populous country and largest economy, is at a defining moment, a moment that has great implications beyond the democratic project and beyond the borders of my

Buhari addresses the Chatham House, February 26 2015;
"Let me assure you that if I am elected president, the world will have
no cause to worry about Nigeria as it has had to recently; that Nigeria
will return to its stabilizing role in West Africa; and that no inch of
Nigerian territory will ever be lost to the enemy because we will pay
special attention to the welfare of our soldiers in and out of service,
we will give them adequate and modern arms and ammunitions to
work with, we will improve intelligence gathering and border controls
to choke Boko Haram's financial and equipment channels, we will be
tough on terrorism and tough on its root causes by initiating a comprehensive economic development plan promoting infrastructural development, job creation, agriculture and industry in the affected
areas."

Photo: International Guardian/File

dear country.

So let me say upfront that the global interest in Nigeria's landmark election is not misplaced at all and indeed should be commended; for this is an election that has serious import for the world. I urge the international community to continue to focus on Nigeria at this very critical moment. Given increasing global linkages, it is in our collective interests that the post-poned elections should hold on the rescheduled dates; that they should be free and fair; that their outcomes should be re-spected by all parties; and that any form of extension, under whichever guise, is unconstitutional and will not be tolerated.

With the fall of the Berlin Wall in 1989, the dissolution of the USSR in 1991, the collapse of communism and the end of the Cold War, democracy became the dominant and most pre-ferred system of government across the globe. That global transition has been aptly captured as the triumph of democracy and the 'most pre-eminent political idea of our time.' On a per-sonal note, the phased end of the USSR was a turning point for me. It convinced me that change can be brought about without firing a single shot.

As you all know, I had been a military head of state in Nige-ria for twenty months. We intervened because we were un-happy with the state of affairs in our country. We wanted to arrest the drift. Driven by patriotism, influenced by the preva-lence and popularity of such drastic measures all over Africa and elsewhere, we fought our way to power. But the global triumph of democracy has shown that another and a preferable path to change is possible. It is an important lesson I have carried with me since, and a lesson that is not lost on the African continent.

In the last two decades, democracy has grown strong roots in Africa. Elections, once so rare, are now so commonplace. As at the time I was a military head of state between 1983 and 1985, only four African countries held regular multi-party elections. But the number of electoral democracies in Africa, according to Freedom House, jumped to 10 in 1992/1993 then to 18 in 1994/1995 and to 24 in 2005/2006. According to the New York Times, 42 of the 48 countries in Sub-Saharan Africa conducted multi-party elections between 1990 and 2002.

The newspaper also reported that between 2000 and 2002, ruling parties in four African countries (Senegal, Mauritius, Ghana and Mali) peacefully handed over power to victorious opposition parties. In addition, the proportion of African countries categorized as not free by Freedom House declined from 59% in 1983 to 35% in 2003. Without doubt, Africa has been part of the current global wave of democratization.

But the growth of democracy on the continent has been uneven. According to Freedom House, the number of electoral democracies in Africa slipped from 24 in 2007/2008 to 19 in 2011/2012; while the percentage of countries categorized as 'not free' assuming for the sake of argument that we accept their definition of "free" increased from 35% in 2003 to 41% in

2013. Also, there have been some reversals at different times in Burkina Faso, Central African Republic, Cote D'Ivoire, Guinea, Guinea-Bissau, Lesotho, Mali, Madagascar, Mauritania and Togo. We can choose to look at the glass of democracy in Africa as either half full or half empty.

While you can't have representative democracy without elections, it is equally important to look at the quality of the elections and to remember that mere elections do not democracy make. It is globally agreed that democracy is not an event, but a journey. And that the destination of that journey is democratic consolidation – that state where democracy has become so rooted and so routine and widely accepted by all actors.

With this important destination in mind, it is clear that though many African countries now hold regular elections, very few of them have consolidated the practice of democracy. It is important to also state at this point that just as with elections, a consolidated democracy cannot be an end by itself. I will argue that it is not enough to hold a series of elections or even to peacefully alternate power among parties.

It is much more important that the promise of democracy goes beyond just allowing people to freely choose their leaders. It is much more important that democracy should deliver on the promise of choice, of freedoms, of security of lives and property, of transparency and accountability, of rule of law, of good governance and of shared prosperity. It is very important that the promise embedded in the concept of democracy, the promise of a better life for the generality of the people, is not delivered in the breach.

Now, let me quickly turn to Nigeria. As you all know, Nigeria's fourth republic is in its 16th year and this general election will be the fifth in a row. This is a major sign of progress for us, given that our first republic lasted five years and three months, the second republic ended after four years and two months and the third republic was a still-birth. However, longevity is not the only reason why everyone is so interested in this election.

The major difference this time around is that for the very first time since transition to civil rule in 1999, the ruling People's Democratic Party (PDP) is facing its stiffest opposition so far from our party the All Progressives Congress (APC). We once had about 50 political parties, but with no real competition. Now Nigeria is transitioning from a dominant party system to a competitive electoral polity, which is a major marker on the road to democratic consolidation. As you know, peaceful alternation of power through competitive elections have happened in Ghana, Senegal, Malawi and Mauritius in recent times. The prospects of democratic consolidation in Africa will be further brightened when that eventually happens in Nigeria.

But there are other reasons why Nigerians and the whole world are intensely focused on this year's elections, chief of which is that the elections are holding in the shadow of huge security, economic and social uncertainties in Africa's most populous country and largest economy. On insecurity, there is a genuine cause for worry, both within and outside Nigeria. Apart from the civil war era, at no other time in our history has Nigeria been this insecure.

Boko Haram has sadly put Nigeria on the terrorism map, killing more than 13,000 of our nationals, displacing millions internally and externally, and at a time holding on to portions of our territory the size of Belgium. What has been consistently lacking is the required leadership in our battle against insurgency. I, as a retired general and a former head of state, have always known about our soldiers: they are capable, well trained, patriotic, and brave and always ready to do their duty in the service of our country.

You all can bear witness to the gallant role of our military in Burma, the Democratic Republic of Congo, Sierra Leone, Liberia, and Darfur and in many other peacekeeping operations in several parts of the world. But in the matter of this insurgency, our soldiers have neither received the necessary support nor the required incentives to tackle this problem. The government has also failed in any effort towards a multi-dimensional response to this problem leading to a situation in which we have now become dependent on our neighbors to come to our rescue.

Let me assure you that if I am elected president, the world will have no cause to worry about Nigeria as it has had to recently; that Nigeria will return to its stabilizing role in West Africa; and that no inch of Nigerian territory will ever be lost to the enemy because we will pay special attention to the welfare of our soldiers in and out of service, we will give them adequate and modern arms and ammunitions to work with, we will improve intelligence gathering and border controls to choke Boko Haram's financial and equipment channels, we will be tough on terrorism and tough on its root causes by initiating a comprehensive economic development plan promoting infrastructural development, job creation, agriculture and industry in the affected areas. We will always act on time and not allow problems to irresponsibly fester, and I, Muhammadu Buhari, will always lead from the front and return Nigeria to its leadership role in regional and international efforts to combat terrorism.

On the economy, the fall in prices of oil has brought our economic and social stress into full relief. After the rebasing exercise in April 2014, Nigeria overtook South Africa as Africa's largest economy. Our GDP is now valued at $510 billion and our economy rated 26th in the world. Also on the bright side, inflation has been kept at single digit for a while and our economy has grown at an average of 7% for about a decade.

But it is more of paper growth, a growth that, on account of mismanagement, profligacy and corruption, has not translated to human development or shared prosperity. A development economist once said three questions should be asked about a country's development: one, what is happening to poverty? Two, what is happening to unemployment? And three, what is happening to inequality?

The answers to these questions in Nigeria show that the current administration has created two economies in one country, a sorry tale of two nations: one economy for a few who have so much in their tiny island of prosperity; and the other economy for the many who have so little in their vast ocean of misery.

Even by official figures, 33.1% of Nigerians live in extreme poverty. That's at almost 60 million, almost the population of the United Kingdom. There is also the unemployment crisis simmering beneath the surface, ready to explode at the slightest stress, with officially 23.9% of our adult population and almost 60% of our youth unemployed. We also have one of the highest rates of inequalities in the world.

With all these, it is not surprising that our performance on most governance and development indicators (like Mo Ibrahim Index on African Governance and UNDP's Human Development Index.) are unflattering. With fall in the prices of oil, which accounts for more than 70% of government revenues, and lack of savings from more than a decade of oil boom, the poor will be disproportionately impacted.

In the face of dwindling revenues, a good place to start the repositioning of Nigeria's economy is to swiftly tackle two ills that have ballooned under the present administration: waste and corruption. And in doing this, I will, if elected, lead the way, with the force of personal example.

On corruption, there will be no confusion as to where I stand. Corruption will have no place and the corrupt will not be appointed into my administration. First and foremost, we will plug the holes in the budgetary process. Revenue producing entities such as NNPC and Customs and Excise will have one set of books only. Their revenues will be publicly disclosed and regularly audited. The institutions of state dedicated to fighting corruption will be given independence and prosecutorial authority without political interference.

But I must emphasize that any war waged on corruption should not be misconstrued as settling old scores or a witch-hunt. I'm running for President to lead Nigeria to prosperity and not adversity.

In reforming the economy, we will use savings that arise from blocking these leakages and the proceeds recovered from corruption to fund our party's social investments programs in education, health, and safety nets such as free school meals for children, emergency public works for unemployed youth and pensions for the elderly.

As a progressive party, we must reform our political economy to unleash the pent-up ingenuity and productivity of the Nigerian people thus freeing them from the curse of poverty. We will run a private sector-led economy but maintain an active role for government through strong regulatory oversight and deliberate interventions and incentives to diversify the base of our economy, strengthen productive sectors, improve the productive capacities of our people and create jobs for our teeming youths.

In short, we will run a functional economy driven by a world-view that sees growth not as an end by itself, but as a tool to create a society that works for all, rich and poor alike. On March 28, Nigeria has a decision to make. To vote for the continuity of failure or to elect progressive change. I believe the people will choose wisely.

In sum, I think that given its strategic importance, Nigeria can trigger a wave of democratic consolidation in Africa. But as a starting point we need to get this critical election right by ensuring that they go ahead, and depriving those who want to scuttle it the benefit of derailing our fledgling democracy. That way, we will all see democracy and democratic consolidation as tools for solving pressing problems in a sustainable way, not as ends in themselves.

Permit me to close this discussion on a personal note. I have heard and read references to me as a former dictator in many respected British newspapers including the well regarded Economist. Let me say without sounding defensive that dictatorship goes with military rule, though some might be less dictatorial than others. I take responsibility for whatever happened under my watch.

I cannot change the past. But I can change the present and the future. So before you is a former military ruler and a converted democrat who is ready to operate under democratic norms and is subjecting himself to the rigors of democratic elections for the fourth time.

You may ask: why is he doing this? This is a question I ask myself all the time too. And here is my humble answer: because the work of making Nigeria great is not yet done, because I still believe that change is possible, this time through the ballot, and most importantly, because I still have the capacity and the passion to dream and work for a Nigeria that will be respected again in the comity of nations and that all Nigerians will be proud of.

I thank you for listening."

Acceptance Speech
(April 1, 2015)

The Die is Cast

Acceptance Statement by General Muhammadu Buhari, GCFR,
President-Elect of the Federal Republic of Nigeria April 1st, 2015

I am immensely grateful to God for this day and for this hour. I feel truly honored and humbled that the Nigerian people have so clearly chosen me to lead them. The official announcement from INEC was the moment the vast majority of Nigerians had hoped and been waiting for.

Today, history has been made, and change has finally come. Your votes have changed our national destiny for the good of all Nigerians. INEC has announced that I, Muhammadu Buhari, shall be your next president. My team and I shall faithfully serve you.

There shall no longer be a ruling party again: APC will be your governing party. We shall faithfully serve you. We shall never rule over the people as if they were subservient to government. Our long night has passed and the daylight of new democratic governance has broken across the land. This therefore is not a victory for one man or even one party. It is a victory for Nigeria and for all Nigerians. Millions of you have worked for this day. So many have risked life and livelihood; and others have died that we may witness this moment

And it is with a very heavy heart that I report many deaths and injuries amidst the jubilations yesterday. We send our sincere condolences to the families and friends of those who lost their lives; and wish speedy recovery to those who suffered injuries. I appeal to all our supporters to celebrate this victory with prayers and reflection instead of wild jubilation.

May the souls of those who died rest in peace. Let us take a moment of silence to honor all of those whose sacrifices have brought us to this fine and historic hour. As the results of the election have shown, their labor has not been and will never be in vain. Democracy and the rule of law will be re-established in the land.

Let us put the past, especially the recent past, behind us. We must forget our old battles and past grievances—and learn to forge ahead. I assure you that our government is one that will listen to and embrace all. I pledge myself and our in-coming administration to just and principled governance. There shall be no bias against or favoritism for any Nigerian based on ethnicity, religion, region, gender or social status.

I pledge myself and the government to the rule of law, in which none shall be so above the law that they are not subject to its dictates, and none shall be so below it that they are not availed of its protection. You shall be able to go to bed knowing that you are safe and that your constitutional rights remain in safe hands. You shall be able to voice your opinion without fear of reprisal or victimization. My love and concern for this nation and what I desire for it extends to all, even to those who do not like us or our politics.

You are all my people and I shall treat every one of you as my own. I shall work for those who voted for me as well as those who voted against me and even for those who did not vote at all. We all live under one name as one nation: we are all Nigerians. Some unfortunate issues about my eligibility have been raised during the campaign. I wish to state that through devotion to this nation, everything I have learned and done has been to enable me to make the best possible contri-bution to public life. If I had judged myself incapable of govern-ing I would never have sought to impose myself on it. I have served in various capacities and have always put in my best. But despite the rancor of the elections, I extend a hand of friendship and conciliation to President Jonathan and his team. I hereby wish to state that I harbor no ill will against anyone. Let me state clearly that President Jonathan has nothing to fear from me. Although we may not agree on the methods of governing the nation, he is a great Nigerian and still our president. He deserves our support and permanent respect by virtue of the office he has held. This is how an honorable nation treats its servants and conducts its affairs; and this is how Nigeria should be. I look forward to meeting with President Jonathan in the days to come to discuss how our teams can make the transition of administrations as efficient as possible.

Here, I want to thank my party for selecting me as its candidate. I thank our party leaders and members for the steadfast contributions they made to bring our dream to fruition. I thank INEC, the police and all other government agencies for performing their tasks in a proper manner and for refusing to be induced to undermine the election and the democratic process. I also wish to thank religious Leaders, traditional leaders, the media, labor unions, Civil Society organizations, organized private sector, youths and students for their roles in this election.

I give special thanks to President Obama and his timely intervention and support for peaceful and credible elections in Nigeria and for sending Secretary John Kerry and other United States officials. The European Union – especially the United Kingdom, France, Germany and other nations that were actively involved in ensuring the success of this election are equally appreciated. My sincere thanks to the United Nations Secretary General Mr. Ban-Ki Moon. The Commonwealth, China, India and other Asian and Gulf states are also hereby appreciated. Finally our brothers in the African Union and ECOWAS have truly and clearly shown and demonstrate their commitment to our democratization process. Former Presidents John Kuffour, Amos Sawyer, Bakili Muluzi and his team are well appreciated. I must also add my appreciation for the role played by civil societies, national and International observers, and other world leaders in ensuring that Nigeria holds free and fair elections.

I assure all foreign governments that Nigeria will become a more forceful and constructive player in the global fight against terrorism and in other matters of collective concern, such as the fight against drugs, climate change, financial fraud, communicable diseases and other issues requiring global response. I want to assure our fellow African nations that Nigeria will now stand as a more constructive partner in advancing the matters of concern to our continent, particularly with regard to economic development and eradication of poverty. Former head of state and President Chief Olusegun Obasanjo, General Yakubu Gowon, Alh. Shehu Shagari, General Ibrahim Babangida, Chief Ernest Shonekan and General Abdulsalami Abubakar deserve commendations for their statesmanship and words of caution and counsel for peace during the tense moments of this electoral period. Most of all, I thank the people of Nigeria for reposing their confidence in me at this trying moment. Our nation wrestles many challenges including insecurity, corruption, and economic decline.

I pledge to give you my best in tackling these problems. The good people of Nigeria, your obligation does not end with casting your ballot. I seek your voice and input as we tackle these problems. This will not be a government democratic only in form. It will be a government democratic in substance and in how it interacts with its own people. No doubt, this nation has suffered greatly in the recent past, and its staying power has been tested to its limits by crises, chief among which is insurgency of the Boko Haram. There is no doubt that in tackling the insurgency we have a tough and urgent job to do. But I assure you that Boko Haram will soon know the strength of our collective will and commitment to rid this nation of terror, and bring back peace and normalcy to all the affected areas. We shall spare no effort until we defeat terrorism.

Furthermore, we shall strongly battle another form of evil that is even worse than terrorism—the evil of corruption. Corruption attacks and seeks to destroy our national institutions and character. By misdirecting into selfish hands funds intended for the public purpose, corruption distorts the economy and worsens income inequality. It creates a class of unjustly-enriched people. Such an illegal yet powerful force soon comes to undermine democracy because its conspirators have amassed so much money that they believe they can buy government. We shall end this threat to our economic development and democratic survival.

I repeat that corruption will not be tolerated by this administration; and it shall no longer be allowed to stand as if it is a respected monument in this nation. I ask you to join me in resolving these and the other challenges we face. Along the way, there will be victories but there may also be setbacks. Mistakes will be made. But we shall never take you for granted; so, be rest assured that our errors will be those of compassion and commitment not of wilful neglect and indifference. We shall correct that which does not work and improve that which does. We shall not stop, stand or idle. We shall, if necessary crawl, walk and run to do the job you have elected us to do.

I realize that the expectation of our people today is as high as their commitment to change has been strong and their belief in us unshaken. While we pledge to begin doing our best without delay, we would like to appeal to them to appreciate the gravity of our situation, so that we become more realistic in our expectations. We will govern for you and in your interests. Your vote was not wasted. This is not the first time Nigerians have cast their votes for us, and this is not the first time they have been counted; but this is the first time that the votes have been allowed to count. With the help of God, we pledge to do our utmost to bring forth the Nigeria you seek.

Thank you for your patience and attention.

General Muhammadu Buhari, GCFR President-Elect, Federal Republic of Nigeria.

Validation of his mandate - **President Muhammadu Buhari takes oath of office during his inauguration. In his address, he said, "A few people have privately voiced fears that on coming back to office I shall go after them. These fears are groundless. There will be no paying off old scores. The past is prologue."**
What has become rather apparent, however, is Buhari's current vindictive approach in fighting graft. This President would be deceiving the populace if he still maintains that he is not hiding under this "War Against Corruption" to settle past scores.

Photo: International Guardian/Archives.

Inaugural
Speech
(May 29, 2015)

Inaugural speech following his swearing-in as President of the Federal Republic of Nigeria on 29th May, 2015

I am immensely grateful to God who has preserved us to witness this day and this occasion. Today marks a triumph for Nigeria and an occasion to celebrate her freedom and cherish her democracy. Nigerians have shown their commitment to democracy and are determined to entrench its culture. Our journey has not been easy but thanks to the determination of our people and strong support from friends abroad we have today a truly democratically elected government in place.

I would like to thank President Goodluck Jonathan for his display of statesmanship in setting a precedent for us that has now made our people proud to be Nigerians wherever they are. With the support and cooperation he has given to the transition process, he has made it possible for us to show the world that despite the perceived tension in the land we can be a united people capable of doing what is right for our nation. Together we co-operated to surprise the world that had come to expect only the worst from Nigeria. I hope this act of graciously accepting defeat by the outgoing President will become the standard of political conduct in the country.

I would like to thank the millions of our supporters who believed in us even when the cause seemed hopeless. I salute their resolve in waiting long hours in rain and hot sunshine to register and cast their votes and stay all night if necessary to protect and ensure their votes count and were counted. I thank those who tirelessly carried the campaign on the social media. At the same time, I thank our other countrymen and women who did not vote for us but contributed to make our democratic culture truly competitive, strong and definitive.

I thank all of you.

Having just a few minutes ago sworn on the Holy Book, I intend to keep my oath and serve as President to all Nigerians.

I belong to everybody and I belong to nobody.

A few people have privately voiced fears that on coming back to office I shall go after them. These fears are groundless. There will be no paying off old scores. The past is prologue.

Our neighbors in the Sub-region and our African brethren should rest assured that Nigeria under our administration will be ready to play any leadership role that Africa expects of it.

Here I would like to thank the governments and people of Cameroon, Chad and Niger for committing their armed forces to fight Boko Haram in Nigeria.

I also wish to assure the wider international community of our readiness to cooperate and help to combat threats of cross-border terrorism, sea piracy, refugees and boat people, financial crime, cybercrime, climate change, the spread of communicable diseases and other challenges of the 21st century.

At home we face enormous challenges. Insecurity, pervasive corruption, the hitherto unending and seemingly impossible fuel and power shortages are the immediate concerns. We are going to tackle them head on. Nigerians will not regret that they have entrusted national responsibility to us. We must not succumb to hopelessness and defeatism. We can fix our problems.

In recent times Nigerian leaders appear to have misread our mission. Our founding fathers, Mr. Herbert Macauley, Dr Nnamdi Azikiwe, Chief Obafemi Awolowo, Alhaji Ahmadu Bello, the Sardauna of Sokoto, Alhaji Abubakar Tafawa Balewa, and Malam Aminu Kano, Chief J.S. Tarka, Mr. Eyo Ita, Chief Denis Osadeby, Chief Ladoke Akintola and their colleagues worked to establish certain standards of governance. They might have differed in their methods or tactics or details, but they were united in establishing a viable and progressive country. Some of their successors behaved like spoilt children breaking everything and bringing disorder to the house.

Furthermore, we as Nigerians must remind ourselves that we are heirs to great civilizations: Shehu Othman Dan fodio's caliphate, the Kanem Borno Empire, the Oyo Empire, the Benin Empire and King Jaja's formidable domain. The blood of those great ancestors flow in our veins. What is now required is to build on these legacies, to modernize and uplift Nigeria.

Daunting as the task may be it is by no means insurmountable. There is now a national consensus that our chosen route to national development is democracy. To achieve our objectives we must consciously work the democratic system. The Federal Executive under my watch will not seek to encroach on the duties and functions of the Legislative and Judicial arms of government. The law enforcing authorities will be charged to operate within the Constitution. We shall rebuild and reform the public service to become more effective and more serviceable. We shall charge them to apply themselves with integrity to stabilize the system.

For their part the legislative arm must keep to their brief of making laws, carrying out over-sight functions and doing so expeditiously. The judicial system needs reform to cleanse itself from its immediate past. The country now expects the judiciary to act with dispatch on all cases especially on corruption, serious financial crimes or abuse of office. It is only when the three arms act constitutionally that government will be enabled to serve the country optimally and avoid the confusion all too often bedeviling governance today.

Elsewhere relations between Abuja and the States have to be clarified if we are to serve the country better. Constitutionally there are limits to powers of each of the three tiers of government but that should not mean the Federal Government should fold its arms and close its eyes to what is going on in the states and local governments. Not least the operations of the Local Government Joint Account. While the Federal Government cannot interfere in the details of its operations it will ensure that the gross corruption at the local level is checked. As far as the constitution allows me I will try to ensure that there is responsible and accountable governance at all levels of government in the country. For I will not have kept my own trust with the Nigerian people if I allow others abuse theirs under my watch.

However, no matter how well organized the governments of the federation are they cannot succeed without the support, understanding and cooperation of labor unions, organized private sector, the press and civil society organizations. I appeal to employers and workers alike to unite in raising productivity so that everybody will have the opportunity to share in increased prosperity. The Nigerian press is the most vibrant in Africa. My appeal to the media today – and this includes the social media – is to exercise its considerable powers with responsibility and patriotism.

My appeal for unity is predicated on the seriousness of the legacy we are getting into. With depleted foreign reserves, falling oil prices, leakages and debts the Nigerian economy is in deep trouble and will require careful management to bring it round and to tackle the immediate challenges confronting us, namely; Boko Haram, the Niger Delta situation, the power shortages and unemployment especially among young people. For the longer term we have to improve the standards of our education. We have to look at the whole field of Medicare. We have to upgrade our dilapidated physical infrastructure.

The most immediate is Boko Haram's insurgency. Progress has been made in recent weeks by our security forces but victory cannot be achieved by basing the Command and Control Centre in Abuja. The command center will be relocated to Maiduguri and remain until Boko Haram is completely subdued. But we cannot claim to have defeated Boko Haram without rescuing the Chibok girls and all other innocent persons held hostage by insurgents.

This government will do all it can to rescue them alive. Boko Haram is a typical example of small fires causing large fires. An eccentric and unorthodox preacher with a tiny following was given posthumous fame and following by his extra judicial murder at the hands of the police. Since then through official bungling, negligence, complacency or collusion Boko Haram became a terrifying force taking tens of thousands of lives and capturing several towns and villages covering swathes of Nigerian sovereign territory.

Boko Haram is a mindless, godless group who are as far away from Islam as one can think of. At the end of the hostilities when the group is subdued the Government intends to commission a sociological study to determine its origins, remote and immediate causes of the movement, its sponsors, the international connections to ensure that measures are taken to prevent a recurrence of this evil. For now the Armed Forces will be fully charged with prosecuting the fight against Boko haram. We shall overhaul the rules of engagement to avoid human rights violations in operations. We shall improve operational and legal mechanisms so that disciplinary steps are taken against proven human right violations by the Armed Forces.

Boko Haram is not only the security issue bedeviling our country. The spate of kidnappings, armed robberies, herdsmen/farmers clashes, cattle rustlings all help to add to the general air of insecurity in our land. We are going to erect and maintain an efficient, disciplined people – friendly and well – compensated security forces within an over – all security architecture.

The amnesty program in the Niger Delta is due to end in December, but the Government intends to invest heavily in the projects, and program currently in place. I call on the leadership and people in these areas to cooperate with the State and Federal Government in the rehabilitation programs which will be streamlined and made more effective. As ever, I am ready to listen to grievances of my fellow Nigerians. I extend my hand of fellowship to them so that we can bring peace and build prosperity for our people.

No single cause can be identified to explain Nigerian's poor economic performance over the years than the power situation. It is a national shame that an economy of 180 million generates only 4,000MW, and distributes even less. Continuous tinkering with the structures of power supply and distribution and close on $20b expanded since 1999 have only brought darkness, frustration, misery, and resignation among Nigerians. We will not allow this to go on. Careful studies are under way during this transition to identify the quickest, safest and most cost-effective way to bring light and relief to Nigerians.

Unemployment, notably youth unemployment features strongly in our Party's Manifesto. We intend to attack the problem frontally through revival of agriculture, solid minerals mining as well as credits to small and medium size businesses to kick – start these enterprises. We shall quickly examine the best way to revive major industries and accelerate the revival and development of our railways, roads and general infrastructure.

You're Excellencies, My fellow Nigerians I cannot recall when Nigeria enjoyed so much goodwill abroad as now. The messages I received from East and West, from powerful and small countries are indicative of international expectations on us. At home the newly elected government is basking in a reservoir of goodwill and high expectations. Nigeria therefore has a window of opportunity to fulfill our long – standing potential of pulling ourselves together and realizing our mission as a great nation.

Our situation somehow reminds one of a passage in Shakespeare's Julius Caesar

There is a tide in the affairs of men which,

Taken at the flood, leads on to fortune;

Omitted, all the voyage of their life,

Is bound in shallows and miseries.

We have an opportunity. Let us take it.

Thank you

Muhammadu Buhari
President Federal Republic of NIGERIA
and Commander in-chief-of the Armed forces

16

SIXTEEN
Author's final thoughts

■ Nigerian leaders through training and knowledge-sharing, must inspire moral character by facilitating discussions on ethics, emphasizing conscientiousness, compassion, and responsibility rather than a traditional reliant on strange rules and government regulations.

Personality Assessment: SWOT

A SWOT (Strength, Weakness, Opportunities, and Threats) analysis, in this context, serves as a tool to investigate fundamental factors that characterize President Buhari's propensity to lead. Organizations use the

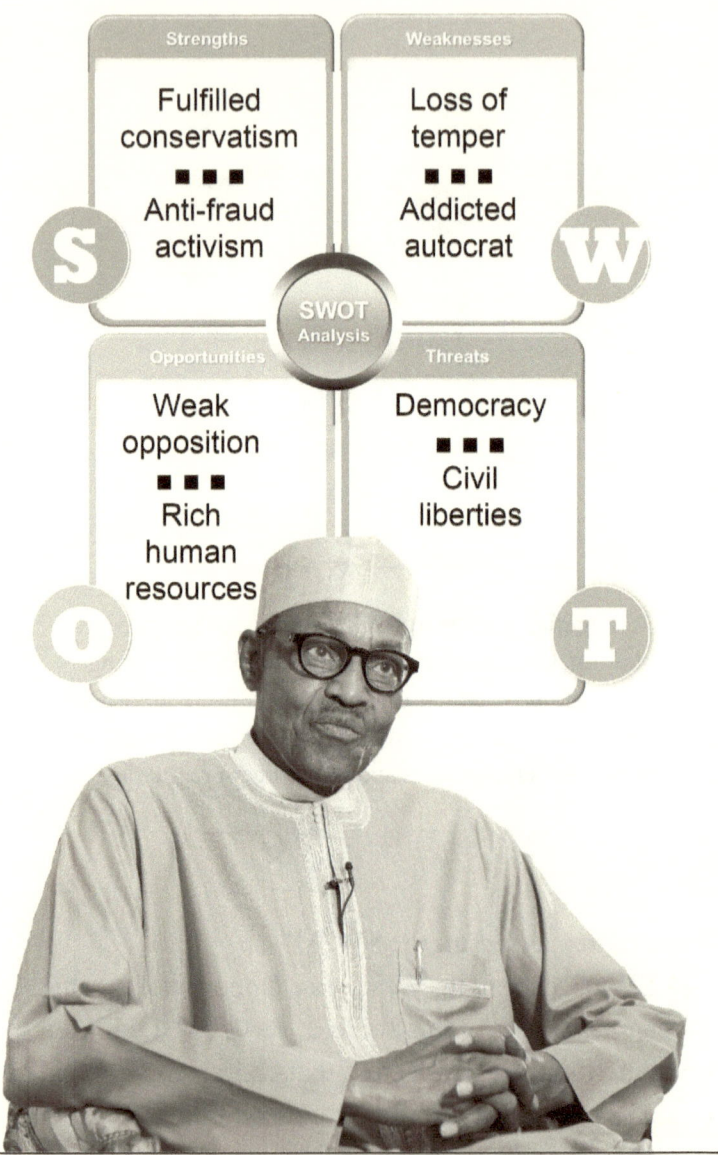

A. Ogbo/American Journal of Transformational Leadership © 2016

SWOT as a factor for developing a strategic plan, including goals, and objectives. President Buhari's strength lies on two major factors; his fulfilled conservative ideology, and undying desire for fighting graft. His weakness, however overwhelms his positive bearings. As a diehard autocrat who often loses his temper to basic issues of management, his team-collaborative attitude remains a concern. On the positive side, with a very weak opposition in his first year in office and abundant human resources in the country's labor force, President Buhari has a good opportunity to turn the tide around. (*See page 136*). There may be also another concern with Buhari's personality. As a former military junta, threats of democracy and civil liberties still hunt his guts, even as he presides over a democratic system.

Buhari's appraisal as a civilian president would fairly cover a twelve-month period of his current stewardship. The appraisal concepts are *idealized influence, inspirational motivation, intellectual motivation, intellectual stimulation, and individualized consideration.

---

*Most decisive assessment of contemporary leadership behavior (Bass, 1999; Bass & Avolio, 1990) were categorized under *Idealized influence, inspirational motivation, intellectual motivation, intellectual stimulation, and individualized consideration.*

Dynamics of leadership effectiveness changed with the emergence of these and other contemporary models. In the transformational model for instance, organizations as Burns (1995) observed, are swift with new ideas, more receptive to competition, and very committed in the renewal process.

(For full references, please see the reference section).

Classification	Assessment
MUHAMMADU BUHARI	
1. Idealized Influence *Propensity to be charismatic*	Raw military training; history of military coups; dictatorship, and forced policies.
2. Inspirational Motivation *Propensity to be inspirational*	Hot-tempered; extremist's beliefs erode motivational spirit
3. Individualized Consideration *Propensity to be considerate*	Hot-tempered, no-second chance policy to public servants; history of worker-retrenchment
4. Intellectual Stimulation *Must be intellectually stimulating*	Authoritative; tyrannical; No evidence-based records of *Intellectual Stimulation*

Comment: One year into his presidency, president Buhari has failed in the capacity to connect with others, develop shared directions, create a secure environment, and allow flexibility for change and innovation. Connecting with others means collaborating with them, uplifting, and encouraging them toward one goal and vision. President Buhari has in fact, distanced himself from the very subordinates he elected as ministers and in other major positions.

President Buhari spent most of his career in an unpolished military community, where authoritative approach inevitably inspires a discouraging tyrannical attitude to leadership. His strength measured negatively on all appraisal factors. For instance, as a leader with idealized influence President Buhari could be trusted and respected. Inspirational motivation describes his ability to motivate and encourage team spirit. His ability to create and innovate through specific challenges defines his intellectual stimulation, whereas individualized consideration would denote his attitude towards coaching or encouraging subordinates to reach specific goals. (*See page 138*).

Unfortunately, one year into his presidency, this president has failed in the capacity to connect with others, develop shared directions, create a secure environment, and allow flexibility for change and innovation. Connecting with others means collaborating with them, uplifting, and encouraging them toward one goal and vision. President Buhari has in fact, distanced himself from the very subordinates he elected as ministers and in other major positions.

His entire leadership circle and connectivity of the three arms of government – Executive, Legislative and Judicial arms – have been in total disarray, as the President himself defies court orders, intimidates the courts, and dictates his own orders. Inspirational motivation,

Leaders and Managers

MANAGERS	Realities of Leadership and Management	LEADERS
Focus on the present		Focus on the future
Maintain status quo and stability		Create change
Implement policies and procedures		Initiate goals and strategies
Maintain existing structure		Culture is based on shared values
Use position power		Use personal power
Transactional: Prioritize tasks and profits		Transformational: Prioritize tasks and emotions

■ Nahavandi, A. (2012). *The art and science of leadership (6th ed.).*
■ Yukl, G. (2013). *Leadership in organizations (8th ed.).*

and individualized consideration of President Buhari becomes another horror movie. His subordinates worship
him in torturing sycophancy. His female subordinates
have to dress in certain ways to suit Buhari's spiritual
beliefs; while they have to sometimes salute him as if he
is still in the military.

Intellectual stimulation means having a leader who inspires innovation and creativity; a leader with a great
measure of critical thinking and problem-solving attitude. In his current designation as the President, Buhari
has not yet shown any determination in enabling innovation or transformation. He named a list of incompatible
subordinates, and left them redundant, (to design their
own Job Descriptions) while he travelled the globe in
name of foreign policy.

Between Leadership and Management

The dynamics of a search and advancement, of leadership effectiveness, has changed with the emergence of
more contemporary approaches to dealing with core
governance challenges. President Buhari always have
believed that leaders are political figures who are there
to fill in positions whereas "technocrats" are obedient,
skilled civil servants who understands the job because
they have been in service for long. He appears to believe that public servant secretaries are more useful to
him than ministers because they would provide the con-

tinuity, dig into the records and then guide him as a novice president.

Again, the President got it all wrong in his naivety about public policy and his inability to distinguish between a leader and manager. This explains why the executive structure of the Nigerian government is in total disorder, submerged in total confusion over the role of leaders and managers. Drawing from two leadership and management scholars, *Gary Yukl* and *Afsaneh Nahavandi,* both the leader and manager have entirely different roles. (*See Table on page 140*).

Renowned management scholar, *John P. Kotter* warned about a scholarly repercussion of using "management" and "leadership" interchangeably. Kotter gave a comprehensive analysis of a distinction between management and leadership. He described Management as a set of basic processes, like planning, budgeting, structuring jobs, staffing jobs, measuring performance and problem-solving, which help an organization to predictably function effectively. Leadership however differs, because it takes an organization into the future, innovatively seeking and exploiting impending opportunities to move the organization to a higher level of success.

By *Kotter's* analysis, the departmental management headed by the Director General in the Nigerian standard could help with the generation of products and services consistent in quality, and on budget, day after day, week after week; whereas the leadership headed by a qualified minister focuses on the organizational vision; about people buying in, about empowerment and, most of all, about producing a useful change. According to *Kotter,* leadership is not about attributes, it's about behavior.

Managing Ethics

Fairness is the most abused leadership concept, especially in regions like Nigeria where the judicial system is peremptorily subjugated by totalitarian headship. *Martin Luther King, Jr.* was absolutely right when he said that injustice anywhere is a threat to justice everywhere. But the current vindictive approach of President Muhammadu Buhari of Nigeria in his attempt to cleanse his country of corruption makes an awkward mockery of his designation, and showcases an absolute lack of knowledge in managing ethics in the public sector.

President Buhari has been passionate with issues of public accountability, and had appointed an anti-corruption advisory committee to guide him on the criminal justice system to enable him confront issues of corruption within the margins of the legal system. As a remedy to a thread of increasing corruption, he has been clamping down on public officers suspected to have looted public fund with arrests, detention, and prosecution; and in some cases, disregarding court others over the justice process.

In fact, this President admitted to defying court orders in granting bail to some of the suspects, citing the gravity of their offences as his reasons for defiance of law and order. While his supporters passionately stand behind him in his mission to cleanse a structure polluted with fraud, the questions about effective strategy and approach to ethical management becomes another issue. Within the framework of the current approach, could mass arrests and detention of suspected looters of public fund , or indiscriminate prosecution of a handful of selected offenders effectively create an ethical public structure?

To maintain an ethical culture and risk management strategies, approach could entail effective programs to raise ethical awareness of public servants. According to management scholars, *Thomas Bateman and Scott Snell,* such programs would provide relevant guidelines and education on ethics, with accessible resources to assist employees in identifying and resolving problems. Ethics programs would range from issues of compliance to integrity and must be designed, not just to punish offenders, but most significantly to detect or prevent violations. Typically components of such program are;

1. Design and implementation of code of ethics
2. Effective ethics training for all public servants
3. Communication of ethical pattern with public servants

4. Composition and implementation of ethical decision-making strategies for public service managers and supervisors.

Finally, I had indicated in my study research, *Phenomenological study of the influence of Nigerian Leadership on the life of its citizens (2015),* that Nigerian leaders through training and knowledge-sharing, must inspire moral character by facilitating discussions on ethics, emphasizing conscientiousness, compassion, and responsibility rather than a traditional reliant on rules and government regulations.

In addition, I had recommended that recognizing the danger signs of ethical lapses can help leaders manage and maintain the ethical culture. As best practices in mitigating lapses, *Bateman – Snell* had suggested major danger signs of what may be deemed as encouraging unethical behavior:

1. Lack of or ineffective code of ethics
2. Passion for short-term solutions to ethical issues
3. Consideration of ethics solely as a legal issue with the least consideration to individual character
4. Lack of explicit ethical procedures
5. Unwillingness of leaders to take ethical stands

Furthermore, if the government could implement a

self-evaluation strategy to predict and prevent these signs, Nigeria could be on a true path to regaining its integrity, both in the continent, and globally.

Managing Transformation

Transformation is not a presidential voyage, it is science. As mentioned earlier in this book, organizational change is not a reshuffle of employees and position; neither is it a mass retrenchment of the workforce to complement the dryness of the treasury. It is a strategic process designed to move the country from the present to a projected future state of economic possibilities and success. This process works faster with an innovative leader who has the vision to progress. Such a leader must be equipped with the attribute, not only to facilitate the process, but also to evaluate and measure performance at all public service sectors.

This leader must establish a process to regulate and improve the transformation process at three performance levels - organization, process, and the workforce. Transformation process without performance evaluation might be fruitless. In the Nigerian system, where redundancy is the bane, an effective change initiative must corroborate performance and feedback. Management and performance evaluation exponents, *Geary Rummler and Alan Brache* warned that implementing a transformation process might not be the end; it is just the beginning; advising that an effective machinery must be established in both the leadership and the public service systems to evaluate performance consistently, or the transformation process would fail.

Is President Buhari ready to embrace the demands of a true change process, or would he continue in his own way, following his current butchery of the praxis of leadership?

References

Bass & Bass (2008). *The Bass Handbook of Leadership: Theory, Research, and Managerial Applications"* 4th edition Free Press

Bass, B. M., and Avolio, B. J. (1994). *Improving organizational effectiveness through transformational leadership.* Thousand Oaks, CA: Sage Publications.

Bass, B. M. (1990). *Bass and Stogdill's handbook of leadership.* New York: Free Press.

Bass, B. M. & Avolio, B. J. (1990). Transformational leadership development: Manual for the Multifactor. *Leadership Questionnaire.* Palo Alto, CA: Consulting Psychologist Press

Bateman, T. S., & Snell, S. A. (2007). *Management: Leading and collaborating in a competitive world* (7th Ed.). Boston, MA: McGraw-Hill/Irwin.

Brown, D. R. (2011). *An experiential approach to organization development* (8th ed.). Boston, MA: Prentice Hall.

Burns, J. A. (1995). Transactional and Transformational Leadership. In J.T. Wren (ed.), *The leader's companion: Insights into leadership through the ages.* New York: The Free Press. [Reprinted courtesy of the *Journal of Contemporary Business, 3*(Autumn1974) published by the School of Business Administration, University of Washington, Seattle, WA.

Burns, J. M. (1978). *Leadership.* New York: Harper & Row

Chemers, M. M. (1995). Contemporary leadership theories. In J.T. Wren (ed.), *The leader's companion: Insights on leadership through the ages.* New York: The Free Press. [Reprinted courtesy of the *Journal of Contemporary Business, 3*(1974).]

Chew, M. (2011). Discover your leadership style. Singapore: Armour Publishing Ltd.

Clawson J.G. (2006). *Level Three Leadership: Getting Below the Surface,* Third Edition, Published by Pearson Prentice Hall. Copyright © 2006 by Pearson Education, Inc.

Coawin R. G. (1972). Strategies for organizational innovation: an empirical comparison *American Sociological Review 1972, Vol. 37* (August):441-454 (EBSCOHOST).

Cuilla J. (1998). *Ethics, the heart of leadership.* Westport, CT: Quorum Books.

DeGeorge, R. T. (2010). *Business ethics* (7th Ed.). Upper Saddle River, NJ: Prentice Hall.

Gallos, J.V. (2006, 2007). *Organization development.* A Francisco, CA; Jossey-Bass.

Johnson, C. E. (Ed.). (2009). *Meeting the ethical challenges of leadership: Casting light or shadow* (3rd Ed). Thousand Oaks, CA: Sage.

Jones, G.R. (2010). *Organizational theory, design, and change* (6th Ed.). Upper Saddle River, NJ: Prentice Hall.

Joseph, C. E. (2012). Corruption and leadership crisis in Africa: Nigeria in focus. *International Journal of Business and Social Science, 3*(11), n/a. Retrieved from http://search.proquest.com/docview/1017542769?accountid=35812

Kotter, J. P. (2015) Management Is (Still) not leadership. *American Journal of Transformational Leadership.* Retrieved from www.ajtlonline.org.

Kuhn, T. (1996). *The structure of scientific revolutions.* Chicago, IL: The University of Chicago Press.

Nadler, David A. and Tushman Michael L. (1995). Beyond the charismatic leader: leadership and organizational change. In *J.T. Wren (ed.), The leader's companion: Insights on leadership through the ages.* New York: The Free Press. [Reprinted courtesy of the *Journal of Contemporary Business, 3*(Autumn 1974).

Nahavandi, A. (2006). *The art and science of leadership.* (4th Ed.). Upper Saddle River, NJ: Pearson.

Ogbo, A. O. (2015). *The influence of leadership.* Houston, TX: Create Space.

Parker, G. (2008). *Team players and teamwork: New strategies for developing successful collaboration, completely updated revised* (2nd Ed.). San Francisco, CA. Jossey-Bass.

Patton, Jr., G. S. (1978). *The Patton Principles.* Province Pub. Co (1978)

Premeaux, S. (2009). The link between management behavior and ethical philosophy in the wake of the Enron convictions. *Journal of Business Ethics, 85*(1), 13-25.

Scott, W.R., Davis, G.F. (2007). *Organizations and organizing.* Upper Saddle River, NJ: Prentice Hall.

Shane, S. (2009). *Technology strategy for managers, and entrepre-neurs,* (1st Ed.). Upper Saddle River, NJ: Pearson.

Wren, J.T. (1995). The leader's companion: *Insights on leadership through the ages.* New York: The Free Press. [Reprinted cour-tesy of the *Journal of Contemporary Business, 3*(Autumn 1974) published by the School of Business Administration, University of Washington, Seattle, WA.

Yukl, G. (2006, 2010). *Leadership in organizations* (7th Ed.). Upper Saddle River, NJ. Pearson Prentice Hall History. (2008).

AMERICAN JOURNAL *of*
TRANSFORMATIONAL LEADERSHIP

Dr. Anthony Obi Ogbo, Ph.D.

Houston resident, Dr. Anthony Obi Ogbo is the publisher of Houston-based *International Guardian,* and the Vice-Chancellor and facilitator of the *American Journal of Transformational Leadership.* He is an author of many books and journals, including *"336 Hours in Nigeria: The Phenomenology of a Broken Nation",* a book on politics, leadership, and psychology.

Dr Ogbo's research interests focus on the fields of management and leadership as they apply to all academic disciplines, including human capital, business administration, organizational leadership, health, applied econometrics, and development economics. His interests are borne out of necessity, to convey the meaning and values of leadership, and facilitate an environment to breed transformational leaders of today for tomorrow's success. His book, *"The Influence of Leadership"* for instance, is a replication of one of his research studies – a phenomenological study of Nigerians living through leadership imperfections. The study results uncovered fundamental leadership gaps in management, discussed the implications, and offered constructive mitigation strategies.

"The Influence of Leadership" for instance, is a replication of one of his research studies – a phenomenological study of Nigerians living through leadership imperfections. The study results uncovered fundamental leadership gaps in management, discussed the implications, and offered constructive mitigation strategies.

One of his latest studies focuses mainly on knowledge-sharing processes in Houston community media organizations and the effects of diversity in teams and groups on performance effectiveness. This study sponsored by the *American Journal of Transformational Leadership* not only aimed at developing relevant approaches to assess knowledge sharing in the team process, but also in exploring intervention strategies to expand and improve them.

Dr. Ogbo is a former president of Houston Association of Black Journalists. With several merit awards to his credit, Ogbo started his media career in 1981 and has worked in various print media companies until 1998 when inaugurated the *International Guardian* in Houston, Texas. In 2004 he established the *Black Senior News*, the first African-American senior newspaper in the state of Texas. Ogbo holds a Master's degree in Human Resources and Human Resources Management, and a Doctorate in Management in Organizational Leadership.

American
Journal of
Transformational
Leadership

www.ajtlonline.org

www.ingramcontent.com/pod-product-compliance
Lightning Source LLC
Chambersburg PA
CBHW020509290526
45786CB00002B/537